MW00698935

BUDDHA

DISCOVERY DECK

53 Sutras and Meditation Cards
to create a silent space within

OSHO

BARNES
&NOBLE
BOOKS
NEW YORK

Buddha Discovery Deck

53 SUTRAS AND MEDITATION CARDS TO CREATE A SILENT SPACE WITHIN

TEXT BY Osho
EDITED BY Carol Neiman
DESIGN BY Bullet Liongson
PHOTOGRAPHS COURTESY OF
Osho Meditation Resort, Pune, India, and private collections.
SPECIAL THANKS TO THE FOLLOWING FOR THEIR
CONTRIBUTIONS OF PHOTOGRAPHY AND EXPERTISE:
Anandadas, Ishana, Zeenat, Shivananda, Anil, and Alexandra.

This edition published by Barnes & Noble, Inc.
by arrangement with OSHO International
©2003 Barnes & Noble

ISBN 0-7607-4584-6
M 10 9 8 7 6 5 4 3 2 1

Contents

How to Use the Cards

The *Buddha Discovery Deck* is a tool to support watchful awareness of the mind, emotions and physical activities in everyday life. These are not "divination cards" — that is, they are not meant to be used for reading the future, or even to interpret what is happening in the present. Rather, they are reminders that each of us carries within ourselves the potential to wake up, to become buddhas in our own right, and that it is this process of awakening that gives meaning and significance to our lives.

There are a total of 53 cards in the deck — one card for each week of the year, plus one, unnumbered "remembrance" card — *Sammasati* — which serves as a reminder that ultimately, the task is to become a light unto ourselves, to fulfill the promise of the buddha within.

Each card carries a photograph of a Buddha statue, a short quotation (sutra) from the body of work known as *The Dhammapada* of Gautam Buddha, and a brief Osho commentary on the sutra. The book corresponds to the deck, and provides more detailed commentary on each card.

The following suggestions are offered for using the entire package:

Before you start using the cards, read the Introduction to the book. This will help you understand the purpose of the text, where it comes from, and how to approach it.

Choose one card at the beginning of each week, with the intention to keep it with you so that you can refer to it often during the day. It might be useful at first to select "trigger" events to help you remember — mealtimes, for example, or your scheduled breaks at work. It is better to keep the card in a place where you must intentionally stop what you are doing, and take it out to look at it. When we leave things "on display" they often become part of the landscape, and we don't notice them anymore.

The cards are numbered to make it easier to find the corresponding text in the book, but they need not necessarily be used in this order. You can also choose them randomly, or according to what words or photographs appeal to you at the moment. Just be sure to put the card aside after the week has passed, so that you are always working with a new one.

Read the section of the book that corresponds to the card you have just chosen. As the week passes, and the words on the card begin to "sink in," you will discover that if you read the text in the book again, it will reveal deeper layers of meaning to you.

After the first couple of days, you will find a rhythm that fits best with your day and allows you to really spend time with the card, to "take a break" and come back to your center of watching. It works best to read the text just as poetry, without making an intellectual effort to understand or analyze it. This allows the words to provoke and wake up the intuitive, wordless understanding that you already carry as a seed within.

Whenever possible during the week, spend some time with your card and re-read the corresponding text in the book, just before you go to sleep. This will allow a deep sense of relaxation and acceptance to permeate your sleep throughout the night. This will be reinforced if you keep the card next to your bed, and look at it again when you wake up in the morning.

Finally, a note about the "remembrance" card (*Sammasati*):

This card is, in a sense, the most important of all. Each of the other cards is pointing toward this one, which is the reminder that waking up and allowing the buddha within to emerge is our most important task in life. It is suggested that you keep this card on top of the deck, and refresh your acquaintance with its message each week before you choose a new card for the week to come.

What Is A Sutra?

A sutra is an essential statement with no elaboration, with no explanation, with no decoration — just the bare, naked core of it. It was needed in ancient days, because people had to remember these sutras. Hence they had to be very condensed, they had to be telegraphic so people could remember for centuries, because they would go from one generation to another just as part of people's memories. Books were not in existence, printing had not come into being. People had to remember; hence the device of the sutra. A sutra means a maxim, just the very essential core. But if you remember it you can always decode it.

And that's what I am doing here — decoding these sutras for you.

In the East, all the great scriptures are written in sutras. Sutra means the most condensed statement, so thin as if it is just a thread — the word sutra literally means a thread. Everything inessential has been cut; only the most essential has been saved. It is the most telegraphic way of expressing things. Hence in the East there are great commentaries. In the West there are no commentaries at all, because in the West no sutras have been written. A sutra needs a commentary.

In the West, the very phenomenon of commentaries has not happened. Nobody comments on Kant, nobody comments on Hegel, nobody comments even on Socrates, nobody comments on the Bible. The very phenomenon of commentaries is absolutely Eastern. And the reason is that the great philosophers of the West came into existence when writing had arrived, when it was not anymore a question of memorizing — you could write a treatise.

And when philosophers like Kant or Hegel or Feuerbach write, they write with all possible implications, complexities, meanings. They also write keeping in mind whether somebody is going to contradict them, what their points might be. They are also keeping in mind what the arguments of the opposite philosophy can be, and they are already replying to them — although nobody has opposed them, nobody has even understood what they are writing about. So their writings are very complete in a way, full and entire. They have not left anything for anybody else to add.

In the East, commentaries started for a certain historical reason. It is at least ten thousand years old — that is the very orthodox view about the history of philosophical development in the East. There are people who think it is far more ancient than ten thousand years. And because there was no writing — printing was not yet invented — every master had to speak in small maxims — not elaborate treatises, but in small sutras. The word sutra means 'the thread'. They are giving you the very minimum to remember, because to remember a vast amount of a great philosophical treatise will not be possible. And there is a danger of forgetting something, there is a danger of adding something of your own. So the way of the sutras was the only possibility — to write in such a condensed way that every disciple of any master could remember the small, seed-like maxims.

But they are only seeds. They indicate the way, they indicate a certain direction. Unless your heart becomes a soil for those seeds, they will not sprout into leaves, into branches, into flowers, into fruits. Those seeds contain everything that is going to happen, they have the whole inbuilt program. If you allow that seed to enter into your being, as it sinks deeper and deeper, you will realize all that is contained in it. It will become a reality in you.

But because individuals are different, because individuals are unique — each individual heart is not the same soil, not the same territory, not the same land — the seed will have to grow according to the soil. Somebody's heart may be very fertile, creative. The tree may become very huge, the foliage may be very green, and when the spring comes there will be thousands of flowers and fruits.

But somebody's heart may be very hard. The seed is the same, but the soil is not going to help the seed much. The seed has to grow against all odds, against all hindrances. The heart is not going to help but on the contrary it will hinder. It is just a seed that has fallen into a land full of stones. It may grow but it won't be the same as if it had fallen in a fertile, creative heart. It may not attain to the same height; it may even be a bit crippled; it may not have much foliage; it may come to only a few flowers.

But the uniquenesses are such — somebody is a poet and the seed may become poetry. And somebody is a musician and the seed may become music. And somebody is a sculptor and the seed may become beauty in stone. It will all depend in which kind of heart the seed falls. And there are many more implications.

It is possible that one heart may be very fertile and it may bring thousands of flowers. And one heart may not be so fertile and it may not bring thousands of flowers but just one flower — very huge, very big. Those thousand flowers will not be in any way competitive to this one flower. In numbers they may be many, but the beauty of this one flower has almost accumulated the whole beauty of thousands of flowers.

I had one gardener with me for many years while I was teaching in the university. I had a beautiful garden. And this old man I had chosen for a certain reason — he was somebody else's gardener, some army officer's gardener. He was winning every year the competition for growing the biggest roses. I used to go to see, because the whole city was involved in the competition.

All the rich people — officers, bureaucrats, professors, doctors, those who could afford a garden — were participants. But I was not interested in the people who were participating. I was interested in finding out who the gardener was, because the poor gardener was not even mentioned when the trophy was given to the winner. It was given to the owner of the garden. I was looking out for the gardener, because this army officer could not be a gardener himself — the poor gardener was not even there.

I followed the officer's car. I looked around his house, I watched, and I found where the gardener was working. When the army officer went in, he did not even tell the gardener, "I have won the trophy because of you. In fact, it belongs to you." He simply went into his garage and then into his house.

I went into his garden. The old man, a poor man, was working. I asked him, "Have you heard that your roses have been chosen as the best for this year?"

He said, "Nobody has told me yet."

I said, "How much is this army officer giving you as salary?"

He said, "Not very much."

I said, "Whatever he is giving, I will give you double. You can tell me later how much he is giving. You just bring whatever you have into my car and come with me."

And then I saw how he was winning…. His whole art was never to allow any rose bush more than one flower. He would cut all the buds and leave only the biggest bud.

I asked him, "What is the secret of it?"

He said, "The secret is simple. The rose bush has a certain amount of juice. It can be distributed in a hundred flowers, but if you don't allow it to be distributed it is bound to assert itself into one flower."

I remained nine years in that city. For nine years continuously this gardener was the winner. And his secret was just to allow one flower to grow. So it is possible — these are the uniquenesses I am talking about — that the same seeds in different hearts will bring different manifestations.

And that is how commentaries began. The master dies, he has thousands of disciples who have listened to him — now they start thinking, what is the significance of a certain statement or of a certain word? In the East it has been a very delicate affair. Not brutal logic, but a very subtle, very feminine art.

Buddha:
A TURNING POINT IN HISTORY

Gautama the Buddha is the greatest breakthrough that humanity has known up to now. Time should not be divided by the name of Jesus Christ; it should be divided by the name of Gautam Buddha. We should divide history before Buddha and after Buddha, not before Christ and after Christ, because Christ is not a breakthrough; he is a continuity. He represents the past in its tremendous beauty and grandeur. He is the very essence of the whole search of man before him. He is the fragrance of all the past endeavors of man to know God, but he is not a breakthrough. In the real sense of the word he is not a rebel. Buddha is, but Jesus looks more rebellious than Buddha for the simple reason that Jesus' rebellion is visible and Buddha's rebellion is invisible.

You will need great insight to understand what Buddha has contributed to human consciousness, to human evolution, to human growth. Man would not have been the same if there had been no Buddha. Man would have been the same if there had been no Christ, no Krishna; there would not have been much difference. Remove Buddha and something of tremendous importance is lost; but his rebellion is very invisible, very subtle.

Before Buddha, the search — the religious search — was fundamentally a concern with God: a God who is outside, a God who is somewhere above in the heavens. The religious search was also concerned with an object of desire, as much as the worldly search was. The worldly man sought money, power, prestige, and the otherworldly man was seeking God, heaven, eternity, truth. But one thing was common: both were looking outside themselves, both were extroverts. Remember this word, because this is going to help you understand Buddha.

Before Buddha, the religious search was not concerned with the within but with the without; it was extrovert, and when the religious search is extrovert it is not really religious. Religion begins only with introversion, when you start diving deeply within yourself.

People had looked for centuries for God: Who is the builder of the universe? Who is the creator of the universe? And there are many who are still living in a pre-Buddha time, who are still asking such questions: Who is the creator of the world? When did he create the world? There are some stupid people who have even determined the day, the date and the year when God created the world. There are Christian theologians who say that exactly four thousand and four years before Jesus Christ — Monday, 1st January! — God created the world or started creating the world, and he finished the job in six days. Only one thing is true about it: that he must have finished the job in six days, because you can see the mess the world is in — it is a six-day job! And since then he has not been heard about. On the seventh day he rested, and since then he has been resting....

Maybe Friedrich Nietzsche is right, that he is not resting — he is dead! He has not shown any concern. Then what happened to his creation? It seems to be completely forgotten. But Christians say, "No, he has not forgotten. Look! He sent Jesus Christ, his only begotten son, to save the world. He is still interested." That is the only interest Christians say he has shown, in sending Jesus Christ...

but the world is not saved. If that was the purpose of sending Jesus Christ to the world, then Jesus has failed and through him God has failed — the world is the same. And what kind of concern was this — his messenger was crucified and God could not do anything?

There are many who are still living in this pre-Buddha worldview.

Buddha changed the whole religious dimension, he gave it such a beautiful turn: he asked real questions. He was not a metaphysician, he never asked a metaphysical question; to him metaphysics was all rubbish. He was the first psychologist the world had known, because he based his religion not on philosophy but on psychology. Psychology in its original meaning means the science of the soul, the science of the within.

He didn't ask who created the world. He asked: "Why am I here? Who am I? Who is creating me?" And it is not a question of the past — who created me — we are constantly being created. Our life is not like a thing created once and for all; it is not an object. It is a growing phenomenon, it is a river flowing. Each moment it is passing through new territory. "Who is creating this life, this energy, this mind, this body, this consciousness, that I am?" His question is totally different. He is transforming religion from extroversion into introversion.

The extrovert religion prays to God; the introvert religion meditates. Prayer is extrovert; it is addressed to some invisible God. He may be there, he may not be there — you can't be sure or certain; doubt is bound to persist. Hence every prayer is rooted somewhere in doubt, in fear, in uncertainty, in greed.

Meditation is rooted in fearlessness, in greedlessness. Meditation is not begging anything from anybody, it is not addressed to anybody. Meditation is a state of inner silence. Prayer is still noise, you are still talking — talking to a God who may not be there. Then it is insane, neurotic; you are behaving in a mad way. Mad people go on talking; they don't bother much whether there is anybody to listen to them or not. That is a sure sign that they are mad — they imagine that somebody is there; not only that, they can almost see the other. Their visualization is great, their imagination is very substantial. They are capable of changing shadows into substance, imagination into realities, fiction into facts. To you they seem to be involved in a monologue; to themselves they are involved in a dialogue. You cannot see who is present there — they are alone — but they see that somebody is there.

It is because of this fact that psychoanalysis is very cautious about religion, because the religious person behaves just like the neurotic. And there are many psychoanalysts who think that religion is nothing but a mass neurosis — and they have a point: the extrovert religion is a mass neurosis.

But psychoanalysts have not yet become aware of Buddha. Buddha will give them a new insight into religion, into true religion. There is no prayer, no God. Meditation is not a dialogue, or even a monologue — meditation is pure silence.

People ask me, "What should the object of meditation be?" They are asking a wrong question, but I can understand why they are asking it. They have lived in the religions of prayer, and prayer cannot be without somebody there to pray to. Prayer needs an object of worship; prayer is a dependence. The worshipper is not independent; he is dependent on the object of his worship and he is afraid also.

But the meditator has no object. Meditation does not mean to meditate upon something. The English word 'meditation' gives a wrong connotation; in English there is no word to translate the

Buddhist word *dhyana*. In fact, in no other language of the world is there a word that is absolutely synonymous with *dhyana*. It is because of this fact that when Buddhism reached China they could not translate it into Chinese; hence *dhyana* became *ch'an* — it is the same word. The Sanskrit word is *dhyana*, but Buddha used Pali, another language, the language that was understood by the people amongst whom he lived. In Pali, *dhyana* becomes *jhana*; from *jhana*, in Chinese it became *ch'an*, and from *ch'an*, in Japanese it became Zen. Chinese had no equivalent, the Japanese had no equivalent. In fact, no other language has any equivalent because no other language has given birth to a man like Buddha. And without a Buddha it is impossible to give this new meaning, this new vision, this new dimension.

In English, meditation means meditating *upon* something; but then it is thinking, at the most contemplation — it is not meditation. Meditation means being meditative, silent, peaceful, with no thoughts in the mind, a consciousness without content. That is the true meaning of meditation: a pure consciousness, a mirror reflecting nothing. When a mirror is not reflecting anything, it is meditation.

Buddha turned the whole religious quest from metaphysics into a great psychology, because he asked: What are the causes of my life and my death? He is not concerned with the universe. He says: We should start from the beginning, and anything, to have a real significance in life, has to be concerned with me myself: Who am I and why am I? What are the causes that go on creating me?

The Buddha Statue
A BLUEPRINT FOR THE INNER

The seers of the ancient East have been very emphatic about the point that all the great arts — music, poetry, dance, painting, sculpture — are all born out of meditation. They are an effort in some way to bring the unknowable into the world of the known for those who are not ready for the pilgrimage — just gifts for those who are not ready to go on the pilgrimage. Perhaps a song may trigger a desire to go in search of the source, perhaps a statue.

The next time you enter a temple of Gautam Buddha or Mahavira, the master of the Jainas, just sit silently and look at the statue. Because the statue has been made in such a way, in such proportions that if you watch it you will fall silent. It is a statue of meditation; it is not concerned with Gautam Buddha or Mahavira.

That's why all those statues look alike — Mahavira, Gautam Buddha, Neminatha, Adinatha, all the twenty-four masters of the Jainas... in the same temple you will find twenty-four statues all alike, exactly alike. In my childhood I used to ask my father, "Can you explain to me how it is possible that twenty-four persons are exactly alike? — the same size, the same nose, the same face, the same body...."

And he used to say, "I don't know. I am always puzzled myself that there is not a bit of difference. And it is almost unheard of — there are not even two persons in the whole world who are alike, what to say about twenty-four?"

But as my meditation blossomed I found the answer — not from anybody else, I found the answer. These statues have nothing to do with the different people. These statues have something to do with what was happening inside those twenty-four people, and that was exactly the same.

And we have not bothered about the outside; we have insisted that only the inner should be paid attention to. The outer is unimportant. Somebody is young, somebody is old, somebody is black, somebody is white, somebody is a man, somebody is a woman — it does not matter; what matters is that inside there is an ocean of silence. In that oceanic state, the body takes a certain posture.

You have observed it in yourself, but you have not been alert. When you are angry, have you observed? — your body takes a certain posture. In anger you cannot keep your hands open; in anger — the fist. In anger you cannot smile — or can you? With a certain emotion, the body has to follow a certain posture. Just small things are deeply related inside.

So those statues are made in such a way that if you simply sit silently and watch, and then close your eyes, a negative shadow image enters into your body and you start feeling something you have not felt before.

Those statues and temples were not built for worshipping; they were built for experiencing. They are scientific laboratories. They have nothing to do with religion. A certain secret science has been used for centuries so the coming generations could come in contact with the experiences of the older generations — not through books, not through words, but through something that goes deeper — through silence, through meditation, through peace.

Origins of the Sutras
THE DHAMMAPADA

These sayings of Buddha are called *The Dhammapada*. This name has to be understood. *Dhamma* means many things. It means the ultimate law, logos. By "ultimate law" is meant that which keeps the whole universe together. Invisible it is, intangible it is — but it is certainly; otherwise the universe would fall apart. Such a vast, infinite universe, running so smoothly, so harmoniously, is enough proof that there must be an undercurrent that connects everything, that joins everything, that bridges everything — that we are not islands, that the smallest grass leaf is joined to the greatest star. Destroy a small grass leaf and you have destroyed something of immense value to the existence itself.

In existence there is no hierarchy, there is nothing small and nothing great. The greatest star and the smallest grass leaf, both exist as equals; hence the other meaning of the word *dhamma*. The other meaning is justice, the equality, the nonhierarchical existence. Existence is absolutely communist; it knows no classes, it is all one. Hence the other meaning of the word *dhamma* — justice.

And the third meaning is righteousness, virtue. Existence is very virtuous. Even if you find something that you cannot call virtue, it must be because of your misunderstanding; otherwise the existence is absolutely virtuous. Whatsoever happens here, always happens rightly. The wrong never happens. It may appear wrong to you because you have a certain idea of what right is, but when you look without any prejudice, nothing is wrong, all is right. Birth is right, death is right. Beauty is right and ugliness is right.

But our minds are small, our comprehension is limited; we cannot see the whole, we always see only a small part. We are like a person who is hiding behind his door and looking through the keyhole into the street. He always sees things...yes, somebody is moving, a car suddenly passes by. One moment it was not there, one moment it is there, and another moment it is gone forever. That's how we are looking at existence. We say something is in the future, then it comes into the present, and then it has gone into the past.

In fact, time is a human invention. It is always now! Existence knows no past, no future — it knows only the present.

But we are sitting behind a keyhole and looking. A person is not there, then suddenly he appears; and then as suddenly as he appears he disappears too. Now you have to create time. Before the person appeared he was in the future; he was there, but for you he was in the future. Then he appeared; now he is in the present — he is the same! And you cannot see him anymore through your small keyhole — he has become past. Nothing is past, nothing is future — all is always present. But our ways of seeing are very limited.

Hence we go on asking why there is misery in the world, why there is this and that...why? If we can look at the whole, all these whys disappear. And to look at the whole, you will have to come out of your room, you will have to open the door...you will have to drop this keyhole vision.

This is what mind is: a keyhole, and a very small keyhole it is. Compared to the vast universe, what are our eyes, ears, hands?

What can we grasp? Nothing of much importance. And those tiny fragments of truth, we become too much attached to them.

If you see the whole, everything is as it should be — that is the meaning of "everything is right." Wrong exists not. Only God exists; the Devil is man's creation.

The third meaning of *dhamma* can be God — but Buddha never uses the word God because it has become wrongly associated with the idea of a person, and the law is a presence, not a person. Hence Buddha never uses the word God, but whenever he wants to convey something of God he uses the word *dhamma*. His mind is that of a very profound scientist. Because of this, many have thought him to be an atheist — he is not. He is the greatest theist the world has ever known or will ever know — but he never talks about God. He never uses the word, that's all, but by *dhamma* he means exactly the same. "That which is" is the meaning of the word God, and that's exactly the meaning of *dhamma*.

Dhamma also means discipline — different dimensions of the word. One who wants to know the truth will have to discipline himself in many ways. Don't forget the meaning of the word discipline — it simply means the capacity to learn, the availability to learn, the receptivity to learn. Hence the word disciple. *Disciple* means one who is ready to drop his old prejudices, to put his mind aside, and look into the matter without any prejudice, without any a priori conception.

And *dhamma* also means the ultimate truth. When mind disappears, when the ego disappears, then what remains? Something certainly remains, but it cannot be called something — hence Buddha calls it nothing. But let me remind you, otherwise you will misunderstand him: whenever he uses the word *nothing* he means no-thing. Divide the word in two; don't use it as one word — bring a hyphen between "no" and "thing," then you know exactly the meaning of nothing.

The ultimate law is not a thing. It is not an object that you can observe. It is your interiority, it is subjectivity.

Buddha would have agreed totally with the Danish thinker, Soren Kierkegaard. He says: Truth is subjectivity. That is the difference between fact and truth. A fact is an objective thing. Science goes on searching for more and more facts, and science will never arrive at truth — it cannot by the very definition of the word. Truth is the interiority of the scientist, but he never looks at it. He goes on observing other things. He never becomes aware of his own being.

That is the last meaning of *dhamma*: your interiority, your subjectivity, your truth.

One thing very significant — allow it to sink deep into your heart: truth is never a theory, a hypothesis; it is always an experience. Hence my truth cannot be your truth. My truth is inescapably my truth; it will remain my truth, it cannot be yours. We cannot share it. Truth is unsharable, untransferable, incommunicable, inexpressible.

I can explain to you how I have attained it, but I cannot say what it is. The "how" is explainable, but not the "why." The discipline can be shown, but not the goal. Each one has to come to it in his own way. Each one has to come to it in his own inner being. In absolute aloneness it is revealed.

And the second word is *pada*. *Pada* also has many meanings. One, the most fundamental meaning, is path. Religion has two dimensions: the dimension of "what" and the dimension of "how." The "what" cannot be talked about; it is impossible. But the "how" can be talked about, the "how" is sharable. That is the meaning of *path.* I can indicate the path to you; I can show you how I have traveled, how I reached the sunlit peaks. I can tell you about the whole geography of it, the whole topography of it. I can give you a contour map, but I cannot say how it feels to be on the sunlit peak.

It is like you can ask Edmund Hillary or Tensing how they reached the highest peak of the Himalayas, Gourishankar. They can give you the whole map of how they reached. But if you ask them what they felt when they reached, they can only shrug their shoulders. That freedom that they must have known is unspeakable; the beauty, the benediction, the vast sky, the height, and the colorful clouds, and the sun and the unpolluted air, and the virgin snow on which nobody had ever traveled before...all that is impossible to convey. One has to reach those sunlit peaks to know it.

Pada means path, *pada* also means step, foot, foundation. All these meanings are significant. You have to move from where you are. You have to become a great process, a growth. People have become stagnant pools; they have to become rivers, because only rivers reach the ocean. And it also means foundation, because it is the fundamental truth of life. Without *dhamma*, without relating in some way to the ultimate truth, your life has no foundation, no meaning, no significance, it cannot have any glory. It will be an exercise in utter futility. If you are not bridged with the total you cannot have any significance of your own. You will remain a driftwood — at the mercy of the winds, not knowing where you are going and not knowing who you are. The search for truth, the passionate search for truth, creates the bridge, gives you a foundation.

These sutras that are compiled as *The Dhammapada* are to be understood not intellectually but existentially. Become like sponges: let it soak, let it sink into you. Don't be sitting there judging;

otherwise you will miss the Buddha. Don't sit there constantly chattering in your mind about whether it is right or wrong — you will miss the point. Don't be bothered whether it is right or wrong.

The first, the most primary thing, is to understand what it is — what Buddha is saying, what Buddha is trying to say. There is no need to judge right now. The first, basic need is to understand exactly what he means. And the beauty of it is that if you understand exactly what it means, you will be convinced of its truth, you will know its truth. Truth has its own ways of convincing people; it needs no other proofs. Truth never argues. It is a song, not a syllogism.

The Cards

[1] HE WATCHES, HE IS CLEAR

The fool sleeps as if he were already dead,
but the master is awake and he lives forever.
He watches. He is clear.

Awareness is eternal, it knows no death. Only unawareness dies.
So if you remain unconscious, asleep, you will have to die again. If
you want to get rid of this whole misery of being born and dying
again and again, if you want to get rid of the wheel of birth and
death, you will have to become absolutely alert. You will have to
reach higher and higher into consciousness.

And these things are not to be accepted on intellectual grounds;
these things have to become experiential, these things have to
become existential. I am not telling you to be convinced
philosophically, because philosophical conviction brings nothing,
no harvest. The real harvest comes only when you make great effort
to wake yourself up.

But these intellectual maps can create a desire, a longing in you;
can make you aware of the potential, of the possible; can make you
aware that you are not what you appear to be — you are far more.

The fool sleeps as if he were already dead, but the master is awake and he lives forever.

He watches.

He is clear.

Simple and beautiful statements. Truth is always simple and always beautiful. Just to see the simplicity of these two statements...but how much they contain — worlds within worlds, infinite worlds. *He watches. He is clear.*

The only thing that has to be learned is watchfulness. Watch! Watch every act that you do. Watch every thought that passes in your mind. Watch every desire that takes possession of you. Watch even small gestures — walking, talking, eating, taking a bath. Go on watching everything. Let everything become an opportunity to watch.

[2] SWIFT AS A RACE HORSE

Mindful among the mindless, awake while others dream. Swift as the race horse, he outstrips the field.

Sleep has to be broken — and when sleep is broken, nobody is awake; only awakening is there. Nobody is enlightened, only enlightenment is there. An enlightened person cannot say "I"; even if he has to use the word it is just a verbal thing, has to be used because of the society. It is just a rule of the language; otherwise he has no "I" feeling.

The world of things disappears — and then what happens? When the world of things disappears, your attachment to things falls, your obsession with things falls. The things themselves don't disappear; on the contrary, things for the first time appear as they are. Then you are not clinging, obsessed; then you are not coloring reality with your own desires, your own hopes and frustrations. Then the world is not a screen for your desires to be projected on. When your desires drop, the world is there but it is a totally new world. It is so fresh, it is so colorful, it is so beautiful! But a mind attached to things cannot see it because the eyes are closed with attachment.

A totally new world arises when the mind disappears, thoughts disappear. It is not that you become mindless — on the contrary you become *mindful*. Buddha uses the term "right mindfulness" all the time. When the mind disappears and thoughts disappear you become *mindful*. You do things — you move, you work, you eat, you sleep, but you are always mindful. The mind is not there, but mindfulness is there. What is *mindfulness*? It is awareness. It is perfect awareness.

[3] STRAYING THOUGHTS

As the fletcher whittles and makes straight his arrows,
    so the master directs his straying thoughts.

There is a famous Tibetan parable:

A man served a master for many, many years. The service was not pure; there was a motivation in it. He wanted a secret from the master. He had heard that the master had a secret — the secret of how to do miracles. With this hidden desire, the man was serving the master day in, day out. He he was afraid to say anything about his motive, but the master was continuously watching him.

One day the master asked, "It is better that you please speak your mind, because I am continuously seeing a motive in all the service that you do for me. It is not out of love, certainly not out of love. I don't see any love in it and I don't see any humility in it. It is a kind of bribery. So please, just tell me, what do you want?"

The man had been waiting for this opportunity. He said, "I want the secret of doing miracles."

The master said, "Then why did you waste your time for so long? You could have told me the very first day you came. You tortured yourself and you tortured me too, because I don't like people around me who have motives. They are ugly to look at. They are basically greedy, and greed makes them ugly. The secret is simple — why didn't you ask me the first day? This is the secret...."

He wrote down a small mantra on a piece of paper, just three lines: "*Buddham sharanam gachchhami. Sangham sharanam gachchhami. Dhammam sharanam gachchhami.*" It means, "I go to the feet of the Buddha; I go to the feet of the Buddha's commune; I go to the feet of the *dhamma*, the ultimate law."

And the master told the man, "You take this small mantra with you, repeat it five times — just five times. It is a simple process. Just remember one condition while you are repeating it — take a bath, close the door, sit silently — and while you are repeating it, don't think about monkeys."

The man said, "What nonsense are you talking about? Why should I think about monkeys in the first place? I have never paid any attention to monkeys in my whole life!"

The master said, "That is up to you, but I have to tell you the condition. This is how the mantra was given to me, with this condition. If you have never thought of monkeys, so far so good. Now go home, and please never come back. You have the secret, you know the condition. Fulfill the condition and you will have miraculous powers, and whatsoever you want to do you can do. You can fly in the sky, you can read people's thoughts, you can materialize things, and so on and so forth."

The man rushed home; he even forgot to thank the master. That's how greed functions; it does not know thankfulness, it does not know gratitude. Greed is absolutely unaware of gratitude; it never comes across it. Greed is a thief, and thieves don't thank people.

The man rushed out, but he was very much puzzled: even on the way home, monkeys started appearing in his head. He saw many kinds of monkeys, small and big, and red-mouthed and black-mouthed, and he was very much puzzled — "What is happening?" In fact he was not thinking of anything else but the monkeys. And they were becoming bigger and they were crowding all around.

He went home, he took a bath, but the monkeys were not leaving him. Now he was becoming suspicious that they were not going to leave him while he was chanting the mantra. He had not even chanted the mantra yet, he was simply preparing. And when he closed his doors, the room was full of monkeys — it was so crowded that he had no space for himself! He closed his eyes and there were monkeys, he opened his eyes and there were monkeys. He could not believe what was happening. The whole night he tried. Again and again he would take a bath, and again and again he would try, and fail, and fail utterly.

In the morning he went to the master, returned the mantra and said, "Keep this mantra with you. This is driving me mad! I don't want to do any miracles, but please help me to get rid of these monkeys!"

It is so impossible to get rid of a single thought! And if you want to get rid of it, it becomes even more difficult, because when you want to get rid of a thought it raises the question — it is a very decisive moment — of who is the master, the mind or you? The mind will try in every possible way to prove that he is the master and not you.

The master has been a slave for centuries, and the slave has been the master for millions of lives. Now the slave cannot leave all his privileges and priorities so easily. He is going to give you great resistance.

You try it! Today take a bath, close your doors, repeat this simple mantra: *Buddham sharanam gachchhami. Sangham sharanam gachchhami. Dhammam sharanam gachchhami* — and don't let the monkeys come to you....

You are laughing at the poor man. You will be surprised: you are that man.

[4] ONLY LOVE DISPELS HATE

In this world, hate never yet dispelled hate.
Only love dispels hate. This is the law,
ancient and inexhaustible.

Something of profound importance: hate exists with the past and the future. Love needs no past, no future. Love exists in the present. Hate has a reference in the past: somebody abused you yesterday and you are carrying it like a wound, a hangover. Or you are afraid that somebody is going to abuse you tomorrow — a fear, a shadow of the fear and you are getting ready, you are getting prepared to encounter it.

Hate exists in the past and the future. You cannot hate in the present — try, and you will be utterly impotent. Try it today: sit silently and hate somebody in the present, with no reference to the past or the future — you cannot do it! It cannot be done; in the very nature of things it is impossible. Hate can exist only if you remember the past. This man did something to you yesterday — then hate is possible. Or this man is going to do something tomorrow — then too, hate is possible. But if you don't have any reference to the past or the future — this man has not done anything to you and he is not going to do anything to you, this man is just sitting there — how can you hate?

But you can love. Love needs no reference; that's the beauty and the freedom of love. Hate is a bondage, hate is an imprisonment — imposed by you upon yourself! And hate creates hate, hate provokes hate. If you hate somebody you are creating hate in that person's heart for you. And the whole world exists in hate, in destructiveness, in violence, in jealousy, in competitiveness. People are at each other's throats — either in reality, actuality, in action, or at least in their minds, in their thoughts, everybody is murdering and killing. That's why we have created a hell out of this beautiful earth — which could have become a paradise.

Love, and the earth becomes a paradise again. And the immense beauty of love is that it has no reference. Love comes from you for no reason at all. It is your outpouring bliss, it is your sharing of your heart. It is the sharing of the song of your being. And sharing is so joyful — hence one shares! Sharing for sharing's sake, for no other motive.

[5] HOW CAN YOU QUARREL?

You too shall pass away.
Knowing this, how can you quarrel?

Aes dhammo sanantano — Buddha repeats this again and again — "this is the eternal law." What is the eternal law? Only love dispels hate, only light dispels darkness. Why? — because darkness in itself is only a negative state; it has no positive existence of its own. It does not exist really — how can you dispel it? You cannot do anything directly to darkness. If you want to do anything to darkness you will have to do something with light. Bring light in and darkness is gone, take light out and darkness comes in. But you cannot bring darkness in or out directly — you cannot do anything with darkness. Remember, you cannot do anything with hate either.

And that's the difference between moral teachers and religious mystics: moral teachers go on propounding the false law. They go on propounding, "Fight with darkness — fight with hate, fight with anger, fight with sex, fight with this, fight with that!" Their whole approach is, "Fight the negative," while the real, true master teaches you the positive law: *aes dhammo sanantano* — the eternal law, "Do not fight with darkness." And hate is darkness, and sex is darkness, and jealousy is darkness, and greed is darkness and anger is darkness.

Bring the light in....

How is the light brought in? Become silent, thoughtless, conscious, alert, aware, awake — this is how light is brought in. And the moment you are alert, aware, hate will not be found. Try to hate somebody with awareness....

These are experiments to be done, not just words to be understood — experiments to be done. That's why I say don't try to understand only intellectually: become existential experimenters. Try to hate somebody consciously and you will find it impossible. Either consciousness disappears, then you can hate; or if you are conscious, hate disappears. They can't exist together.

[6] BEYOND JUDGMENTS

A mind beyond judgments
Watches and understands.

Don't consider what is right and what is wrong, because if you consider what is right and what is wrong you will be divided, you will become a hypocrite. You will pretend the right and you will do the wrong. And the moment you consider what is right and what is wrong, you become attached, you become identified. You certainly become identified with the right.

For example, you see on the side of the road a hundred-dollar bill; it may have fallen from somebody's pocket. Now the question arises: To take it or not to take it? One part of you says, "It is perfectly right to take it. Nobody is looking, nobody will ever suspect. And you are not stealing — it is just lying there! If you don't take it, somebody else is going to take it anyway. So why miss it? It is perfectly right!"

But another part says, "This is wrong — this money does not belong to you, it is not yours. In a way, in an indirect way, it is stealing. You should inform the police, or if you don't want to be bothered with it, then go ahead, forget all about it. Don't even look back. This is greed and greed is a sin."

Now, these two minds are there. One says, "It is right, take it," the other says, "It is wrong, don't take it." With which mind are you going to identify yourself? You are certainly going to identify with the mind that says it is immoral, because that is more ego satisfying: "You are a moral person, you are not ordinary; anybody else would have taken the hundred-dollar bill. In such times of difficulty, people don't think of such delicacies." You will identify yourself with the moral mind. But there is every possibility you will take the money. You will identify yourself with the moral mind, and you will disidentify yourself from the mind that is going to take the money. You will condemn it deep down; you will say, "It is not right — it is the sinner in me, the lower part, the condemned part." You will keep yourself aloof from it. You will say, "I was against it. It was my instinct, it was my unconscious, it was my body, it was my mind that persuaded me to do it; otherwise, I knew that it was wrong. I am the one who knows that it was wrong."

You always identify yourself with the right, the moralistic attitude, and you disidentify from the immoral act — although you do it! This is how hypocrisy arises.

To go beyond judgments of good and bad is the way of watchfulness. And it is through watchfulness that transformations happen. This is the difference between morality and awareness. Morality says, "Choose the right and reject the wrong. Choose the good and reject the bad." Awareness says, "Simply watch both. Don't choose at all. Remain in a choiceless consciousness."

[7] A FOOL INDEED

The fool who knows he is a fool is that much wiser.
The fool who thinks he is wise is a fool indeed.

The fool is always concerned with only one thing — his ego. Anything that nourishes his ego is good — anything — and he is ready to cling to it. The fool even clings to misery, because it is his misery. He goes on accumulating whatsoever he can get, because the fool has no idea of his inner kingdom, of his inner treasures. He goes on accumulating junk because he thinks this is all that can be possessed. Junk outside and junk inside — that's what people go on collecting. Things they collect, and thoughts they collect. Things are junk outside, thoughts are junk inside, and you are drowned in your junk.

Have a look, a dispassionate, detached look at your life, what you have been doing with it, and what you have got out of it. And don't try to fool yourself, because this is how mind goes on.

Unless you have something that you can take beyond death, remember, you don't have anything at all — your hands are empty. Unless you have something deathless, eternal, you are a fool.

[8] NEITHER PRAISE NOR BLAME

The wind cannot shake a mountain.
Neither praise nor blame moves the wise man.

To be wise is not to be knowledgeable. To be wise means to realize something of your consciousness — first within and then without; to feel the pulsation of life within you and then without. To experience this mysterious consciousness that you are, first one has to experience it in the innermost core of one's being, because that is the closest door to the universal consciousness.

Once you have known it within, it is not difficult to know it without. But remember: the wise man never accumulates knowledge — his wisdom is spontaneous. Knowledge always belongs to the past, wisdom belongs to the present.

Remember these distinctions. Unless you understand the difference very clearly between knowledge and wisdom, you will not be able to understand these sutras of Gautama the Buddha. And they are tremendously important.

Knowledge satisfies the ego; wisdom destroys the ego completely; hence people seek knowledge. It is very rare to find a seeker who is not interested in knowledge but is committed to wisdom. Knowledge means theories about truth; wisdom means truth itself. Knowledge means secondhand; wisdom means firsthand. Knowledge means belief: others say it and you believe. And all beliefs are false! No belief is ever true. Even if you believe in the word of a Buddha, the moment you believe it is turned into a lie.

Truth cannot be believed; either you know or you don't know. If you know, there is no question of belief; if you don't know, there is again no question of belief. If you know, you know; if you don't know, you don't know.

Belief is a projection of the tricky mind — it gives you the feeling of knowing, without knowing. You can easily believe in God, you can easily believe in immortality of the soul, you can easily believe in the theory of reincarnation. In fact, they remain just superficial; deep down you are not affected by them, not at all. When death knocks at your door you will know that your beliefs have all disappeared. The belief in the immortality of the soul will not help you when death knocks at your door — you will cry and weep and you will cling to life. When death comes you will forget all about God; you will not be able to remember the complicated implications of the theory of reincarnation. When death knocks, it knocks down the whole structure of knowledge that you had built around yourself. It leaves you absolutely empty... and with the awareness that the whole of life has been a wastage.

Wisdom is a totally different phenomenon. It is experience, not belief. It is existential experience, it is not "about." You don't believe in God — you know God. You don't believe in the immortality of the soul, you have tasted it. You don't believe in reincarnation — you remember that you have been in many bodies; you have been a rock, you have been a tree, you have been animals, birds, you have been a man, a woman... you have lived in so many forms. You see that only the superficial changes; the essential is eternal.

This is seeing, not believing. And all the real masters are interested to help you to see, not to make you believe.

Wisdom arises within you, it is not a scripture. You start reading your own consciousness — and there are hidden all the Bibles and all the Gitas and all the Dhammapadas.

[9] UNTOUCHED, UNATTACHED...

Happiness or sorrow—whatever befalls you,
walk on untouched, unattached.

It will be of great importance if some day in the future we start changing the patterns of our languages, because our languages are very deeply rooted in ignorance. When you feel hungry, you immediately say, "I am hungry." That creates an identification and gives you a feeling as if you are hungry. You are not. Language should be such that it does not give you this wrong notion — "I am hungry." What is really the case is that you are observing that the body is hungry; you are watching the fact that the stomach is empty, that it desires food — but this is not you. You are the watcher. You are always the watcher, you are never the doer. You always go on standing as a watcher far away.

Get more and more rooted into watching — that's what Buddha calls *vipassana*, insight. Just see with inner eyes whatsoever happens, and remain untouched, unattached.

A tough, old-time Indian fighter came straggling back into camp with seven arrows piercing his chest and legs.

A doctor examined him and remarked, "Amazing stamina. Don't they hurt?"

The oldtimer grunted, "Only when I laugh."

In fact, they should not hurt even then — and they don't hurt to a Buddha. Not that if you pierce the Buddha with an arrow there is no hurt; the hurt is there. He may feel it even more than you, because a Buddha's sensitivity is at the optimum — you are insensitive, dull, half dead. The scientists say that you only allow two percent of

information to reach you; ninety-eight percent is kept outside of you, your senses don't allow it in. Only two percent of the world reaches you; ninety eight percent is excluded. To the buddha, a hundred percent of the world is available, so when an arrow pierces a buddha it hurts a hundred percent. To you it hurts only two percent.

But there is a great difference: a buddha is a watcher. It hurts, but it does not hurt *him*. He watches as if it is happening to somebody else. He feels compassion for the body — he feels compassion, has compassion for his body — but he knows that he is not the body. He takes every possible care because he respects the body. It is such a beautiful servant, it is such a good house to live in — he takes care but he remains aloof.

Even when the body is dying a buddha goes on watching. His watchfulness remains to the very last. The body dies and the buddha goes on watching that the body has died. If one can watch to such an extent, one goes beyond death.

[10] IN THE EMPTY FOREST

Even in the empty forest he finds joy
because he wants nothing.

All great values of life grow in the climate of freedom; hence freedom is the most fundamental value and also the highest pinnacle. If you want to understand Buddha you will have to taste something of the freedom he is talking about.

His freedom is not of the outside. It is not social, it is not political, it is not economic. His freedom is spiritual. By "freedom" he means a state of consciousness unhindered by any desire, unchained to any desire, unimprisoned by any greed, by any lust for more. By "freedom" he means a consciousness without mind, a state of no-mind. It is utterly empty, because if there is something, that will hinder freedom; hence its utter emptiness.

This word "emptiness" — *shunyata* — has been very much misunderstood by people, because the word has a connotation of negativity. Whenever we hear the word "empty" we think of something negative. In Buddha's language, emptiness is not negative; emptiness is absolutely positive, more positive than your so-called fullness, because emptiness is full of freedom; everything else has been removed. It is spacious; all boundaries have been dropped. It is unbounded — and only in an unbounded space, freedom is possible. His emptiness is not ordinary emptiness; it is not only absence of something, it is a presence of something invisible.

For example, when you empty your room. As you remove the furniture and the paintings and the things inside, the room becomes empty on the one hand, but on the other hand something invisible starts filling it. That invisibleness is "roominess," spaciousness; the room becomes bigger. As you remove the things, the room is becoming bigger and bigger. When everything is removed, even the walls, then the room is as big as the whole sky.

That's the whole process of meditation: removing everything; removing yourself so totally that nothing is left behind — not even you. In that utter silence is freedom. In this utter stillness grows the one-thousand-petaled lotus of freedom. And great fragrance is released: the fragrance of peace, compassion, love, bliss.

[11] HOLLOW WORDS

> Better than a thousand hollow words
> is one word that brings peace.

A famous story:

One night the great German philosopher, Professor Von Kochenbach, saw two doors in a dream, one of which led directly to love and paradise, and the other to an auditorium where a lecture was being given on love and paradise. There was no hesitation on Von Kochenbach's part — he darted in to hear the lecture.

The story is significant. It is fictitious, but not so fictitious really. It represents the human mind: it is more interested in knowledge than in wisdom, it is more interested in information than transformation. It is more interested to know about beauty, truth and love than to experience beauty, truth, and love.

On the surface it looks logical: first one has to become acquainted with what paradise is, only then can one enter paradise. First you have to have a map. Logical, still stupid; logical only in appearance, but deep down utterly unintelligent.

Love does not need you to have information about it because it is not something outside you, it is the very core of your being. You have already got it, you have only to allow it to flow. Paradise is not somewhere else so that you need a map to reach there. You are in paradise, only you have fallen asleep. All that is needed is an awakening.

An awakening can be immediate, awakening can be sudden — in fact, awakening can only be sudden. When you wake somebody up, it is not that slowly slowly, in parts, gradually, he wakes up. It is not that now he is ten percent awake, now twenty, now thirty, now forty, now ninety-nine, now ninety-nine point nine, and then a hundred percent — no. When you shake a sleepy person, he awakes immediately. Either one is asleep or one is awake; there is no place in between.

But people keep clinging to words — words that are hollow, words that carry no meaning, words that have no significance, words that have been uttered by people as ignorant as you are. Maybe they were educated, but education does not dispel ignorance. Knowing about light is not going to dispel darkness. You can know all that is available in the world about light; you can have a library in your room consisting only of books on light, yet that whole library will not be able to dispel the darkness. To dispel the darkness you will need a small candle — that will do the miracle.

[12] CONQUER YOURSELF

> It is better to conquer yourself than to win
> a thousand battles. Then the victory is yours.
> It cannot be taken from you, not by angels
> or by demons, heaven or hell.

There are just a few very significant events in the life of Alexander the Great. One is the meeting with the great mystic, Diogenes. Diogenes was lying naked on the bank of a river taking a sunbath. It was early morning... and the early sun and the beautiful riverbank and the cool sand. And Alexander was passing by; he was coming to India.

Somebody told him, "Diogenes is just close by — and you have always been inquiring about Diogenes" — because Alexander had heard many stories. Diogenes was really a man worth calling a man! Even Alexander, deep down, was jealous of him.

He went to see him. He was impressed by his beauty — naked, undecorated, with no ornaments. Alexander himself was covered in ornaments, decorated in every possible way, but he looked very poor before Diogenes. And he said to Diogenes, "I feel jealous of you. I look poor compared to you — and you have nothing! What is your richness?"

Diogenes said, "I don't desire anything — desirelessness is my treasure. I am a master because I don't possess anything — nonpossessiveness is my mastery, and I have conquered the world because I have conquered myself. And my victory is going with me, and your victory will be taken away by death."

And when Alexander was dying he remembered Diogenes, his laughter, his peace, his joy. He remembered that Diogenes had something that goes beyond death, and he realized, "I have nothing." He wept, tears came to his eyes, and he said to his ministers, "When I die and you carry my body to the cemetery, let my hands hang out of the casket."

The ministers asked, "But this is not the tradition! Why? Why such a strange request?"

Alexander said, "I would like people to see that I came empty-handed and I am going empty-handed, and all my life has been a waste. Let my hands hang out of the casket so everybody can see — even Alexander the Great is going empty-handed."

[13] QUICK TO DO GOOD

Be quick to do good. If you are slow,
the mind, delighting in mischief, will catch you.

Buddha says, Be quick to do good.

Why "be quick"? Why do it immediately? Mind will say, "Tomorrow. Wait. Let us think about it." And thinking never comes to any conclusion, remember; thinking has never come to any conclusion. Ten thousand years of philosophizing and there is not a single conclusion in philosophy. They have not arrived at any truth; they are still continuing. The same arguments go on being repeated in different forms and different ways, and philosophy goes on moving in a vicious circle. The philosopher remains inconclusive, and to remain inconclusive your whole life means not to live at all.

Life is possible only out of decisiveness, out of commitment, involvement; otherwise you are always a spectator, you never participate in anything.

The mind is very much afraid of saying yes and the mind is very much afraid of doing good, because the good can be done only in a state of egolessness. The good is a by-product of a state of no-mind. Try to understand it — and when I say try to understand it I am not saying try to think it over. I am simply saying, listen from the heart, with a loving heart.

These sutras can be understood only by the heart. They have come out of the greatest heart that has lived on the earth, and they can be understood only by the heart.

[14] ALL LOVE LIFE

> *All beings tremble before violence.*
> *All fear death. All love life.*

Violence is something against nature. The aware person cannot be violent — not that he practices nonviolence, remember. If you practice nonviolence you will become a Gandhian, a phony. The Gandhian is not an aware person. He practices nonviolence, he *tries* to become nonviolent. He has no understanding. He creates a character, but deep down he has no consciousness that can function as a center of that character.

The mystic first creates the consciousness; then the character follows of its own accord. The moralist creates the character, but consciousness does not follow the character. Character is a very superficial thing.

All beings tremble before violence. All fear death. All love life. There is no need to prove these things. These are simple observations, evident to everybody. But a few conclusions can be drawn from them. If all beings tremble before violence, then there is something wrong in violence, basically wrong. It is against nature.

Destructiveness is not natural — to be creative is natural. Not violence but compassion is natural, not violence but love. Not anger, not hate, because those are the things that lead to violence, those are the seeds. Love, compassion, sharing, these are natural. And to be natural is to be religious.

All fear death; hence, do not kill. Rather, help people to know death. Their fear is because of ignorance. They are afraid of death because death is the greatest unknown. There is no way to know death unless you die. Help people to know death through meditation, because that is a way of dying and still remaining alive.

All love life; hence, love. Create contexts, spaces, where more love can grow. Create a space where your love energies can flow, where they have no hindrance, no obstructions.

[15] BURN AND BE SWIFT

Like a noble horse, smart under the whip,
burn and be swift.

Buddha was a prince before he became enlightened, and when he was a prince he really loved horses. He was a lover of horses. In those days, horses were the greatest support in war.

When he became enlightened he referred to horses many times, in many ways. He says there are four kinds of horses. First, the worst: even if you beat them, the more you beat, the more stubborn they become. They have no aristocracy, no grace, no dignity. You can insult them, you can whip them, you can beat them — they are very thick-skinned. If they don't want to move, they will not move.

Then the second kind: if you beat them they will move; they have a little dignity, a sense of self-honor. Then the third kind, a little higher: you need not beat them — just the noise of the whip is enough. And the highest, the fourth: even the noise of the whip is not needed — only the shadow of the whip is enough.

Buddha says that people are also of four kinds. The highest, the most intelligent, the real seekers of truth, only need the shadow of the whip; just a little hint from the master is enough. Buddha says: A noble horse rarely feels the touch of the whip. There is no need for the noble horse to feel the touch of the whip — just the shadow.

Be like a noble horse — smart, aware, watchful.

[16] THE IGNORANT MAN

The ignorant man is an ox.
He grows in size, not in wisdom.

The most fundamental question before Gautama the Buddha was, "What is wisdom?" And the same is true for everyone. Down the ages the sages have been asking, "What is wisdom?" If it can be answered by you, authentically rooted in your own experience, it brings a transformation of life.

You can repeat the definitions of wisdom given by others, but they won't help you. You will be repeating them without understanding them, and that is one of the pitfalls to be avoided on the path. Never repeat what you have not experienced yourself. Avoid knowledge, only then can you grow in wisdom.

Knowledge is something borrowed from others, wisdom grows in you. Wisdom is inner, knowledge outer. Knowledge comes from the outside, clings to your surface, gives you great pride and keeps you closed, far far away from understanding. Understanding cannot be studied; nobody can teach it to you. You have to be a light unto yourself. You have to seek and search within your own being, because it is already there at the very core. If you dive deep you will find it. You will have to learn how to dive within yourself — not in the scriptures, but within your own existence.

The taste of your own existence is wisdom. Wisdom is experience, not information.

[17] STRAIGHTEN YOURSELF

To straighten the crooked you must first do a harder thing—straighten yourself.

It is easy to look at other people's faults. One loves to see other people's faults because that helps and strengthens your ego: "I am far superior." It is very difficult to see one's own faults; only a man who loves himself can see them.

Don't listen to others, what they say about you. See yourself, who you are, where you are, what your faults are. And the miracle is that seeing a fault through your own awareness dissolves it. You need not make any effort to dissolve it; the very awareness is enough. It starts melting like ice in the hot sun.

But it is very difficult to see one's own faults, because you never look at yourself; you are constantly extroverted, looking at others.

The shapely new stenographer gave a piece of paper to the company auditor, saying, "Here is that report you wanted, Mr. Berry."

"My name is Mr. Perry!" he corrected. "You must have been talking to the head bookkeeper who can't pronounce his P's right. Did he say anything about me?"

"Only that when it comes to meaningless details, you are a regular brick!"

It is certainly difficult, because you have to turn your whole consciousness towards yourself. And we have become so extroverted, we have been made so extroverted that introversion seems to be

almost impossible. We are paralyzed; we can look only at others. Even if we want to look at ourselves we have to look in a mirror. Then the image in the mirror becomes the other.

One has to learn to look at oneself with closed eyes, to watch silently. And don't carry any a priori prejudices. Many people have told you, "These are your faults." Don't carry those ideas within you, otherwise you will find them — because thought is very inventive. Put aside all that has been said about you. Remember only one thing: unless you know it on your own authority, it has no value, no meaning.

So go without any prejudice — for or against. Just go in total openness and see. And if you are loving and if you know how to watch, you will come across the most mysterious phenomenon: seeing a fault is dissolving it. That is Buddha's great secret: knowing that you are doing something wrong is enough; you can't do it anymore.

[18] YOU ARE THE SOURCE

> Mischief is yours. Sorrow is yours.
> But virtue also is yours. And purity.
> You are the source of all purity and all impurity.

A completely transformed human being is born the moment you accept your responsibility for yourself, the moment you say, "Whatsoever I am is my choice — not of the past but of the present. It is my choice of this moment, and if I want to change it I am absolutely free to change it. Nobody can hinder me — no social force, no state, no history, no economics, no unconscious, can hinder me. If I am determined to change it, I can change it."

Yes, in the beginning the responsibility looks like a heavy, heavy weight. It feels good to throw the responsibility on somebody else. At least you can enjoy this much, that "I am not responsible." You can enjoy that you are just a victim, helpless. In the beginning, to accept responsibility for yourself totally and unconditionally is heavy. It creates despair, anguish, anxiety — but only in the beginning. Once it is accepted, slowly you become aware of the great potential and the great freedom that it brings.

If I am responsible for my misery, that also means, automatically, that I am responsible for my bliss. If I am responsible for my misery, I can stop it *immediately*. Let me repeat the word immediately — not even for a single moment does one have to wait. It is not a question of changing your past lives, it is not a question of changing the whole society, it is not a question of bringing in the dictatorship of the proletariat, and it is not a question of going into years and years of psychoanalysis. It is a simple question of accepting the responsibility that "Whosoever I am, I have created my climate, my being."

Man is born only as a potential. He can become a thorn for himself and for others, he can also become a flower for himself and for others. And remember, whatsoever you are for others you are for yourself too, and whatsoever you are for yourself you are for others too. If you are a flower to yourself, your fragrance is bound to be released; it will reach others. If you are a thorn to yourself, how can you be a flower to others?

[19] OUTSIDE THE LAW

*Do not live in the world in distraction
and false dreams, outside the law.*

Your mind is continuously creating distractions. Just watch your mind, and you will understand what Buddha is saying. It never allows you to sit silently even for a few moments. If you sit silently it says, "Why not listen to the radio? The newspaper must have come, the mail may have arrived. Why not go to the movie? Why not watch TV?" If you are in the shop your mind says, "Go home, rest — you are tired." If you are at home your mind says, "What you are doing here, wasting your time? Go to the shop — you could have earned something!"

The mind never allows you to be where you are, it never allows you to see things as they are. It is always taking you somewhere else, either into the past or into the future; it never allows you to be in the present. Either it drags you into memories — which are nothing but footprints on the sands of time — or it drags you into the future: great projections, great expectations, desires, goals…. And you become so much involved with them — as if they have some reality! And the reality is slipping out of your hands while you are engaged in all these trips into the past, into the future.

The mind never allows you and will never allow you to see that which is; it always takes you to that which is not.

One of the names of Buddha is *Tathagata* — one who lives in suchness, one who has become free from all the distractions of the mind. And the miracle is that the mind consists only of distraction, so once you are free of all distractions there is no mind left. In the present there is no mind. In the present there is only consciousness, awareness, watchfulness.

Live in the world, but not through the mind. Don't let the past or the future stand between you and reality. And if you can manage the state of no-mind even for a few moments — that's what meditation is all about — you will be surprised: suddenly you are in rhythm with existence. You will know what Buddha calls *aes dhammo sanantano* — the eternal law.

[20] THE SIMPLE TEACHING

> Master yourself according to the law.
> This is the simple teaching of the awakened.

"According to the law" does not mean the law of the state or the law given by the priests. "According to the law" for Buddha means according to the ultimate law of life and existence.

There is a tremendous harmony — anybody just a little bit sensitive, intelligent, can feel it — life is a harmonious whole. It is not a chaos, it is a cosmos. Why is it not a chaos? — because a law runs through and through it like a thread in a garland. That thread is invisible, you see only the flowers, but that thread is keeping them together. Existence is a garland; there is a thread, a sutra — sutra means thread — a very thin thread, almost invisible, running through the whole existence, that makes it a cosmos instead of a chaos.

"According to the law" in the words of Buddha means: Be in harmony with nature, existence. Don't fight with it, don't go against it. Don't try to go upstream, to flow upstream. To be in a let-go with existence is to follow the law. *aes dhammo sanantano* — this is the

inexhaustible law. If you relax, if you allow the law to take you over, to possess you, you will be overflooded with it. You need not go on an ego trip. The river is already flowing to the ocean — you simply flow with the river. No need to swim either — float, and you will reach the ocean.

[21] JOYFULLY

He who wishes to awake consumes his desires joyfully.

What does Buddha mean by "desire"? Desire means your whole mind. Desire means not to be here now. Desire means moving somewhere in the future which is not yet. Desire means a thousand and one ways of escaping from the present. Desire is equivalent to mind. In Buddha's terminology, desire is mind.

And desire is time too. When I say desire is time too, I don't mean the clock time, I mean the psychological time. How do you create future in your mind? — by desiring. You want to do something tomorrow — you have created the tomorrow; otherwise the tomorrow is nowhere yet, it has not come.

The man who lives in the future, lives a counterfeit life. He does not really live, he only pretends to live. He hopes to live, he desires to live, but he never lives. And the tomorrow never comes, it is always today. And whatsoever comes is always now and here, and he does not know how to live now-here; he knows only how to escape from now-here. The way to escape is called "desire," *tanha* — that is Buddha's word for what is an escape from the present, from the real into the unreal.

The man who desires is an escapist.

Now, this is very strange, that meditators are thought to be escapists. That is utter nonsense. Only the meditator is not an escapist — everybody else is. Meditation means getting out of desire, getting out of thoughts, getting out of mind. Meditation means relaxing in the moment, in the present. Meditation is the only thing in the world that is not escapist, although it is thought to be the most escapist thing. People who condemn meditation always condemn it with the argument that it is escape, escaping from life. They are simply talking nonsense; they don't understand what they are saying.

Meditation is not escaping from life: it is escaping *into* life. Mind is escaping from life, desire is escaping from life.

[22] AMONG THE TROUBLED

Live in joy, in peace,
even among the troubled.

You cannot change the whole world. You have a small lifespan, it will be gone soon. You cannot make it a condition that "I will rejoice only when the whole world has changed and everybody is happy." That is never going to happen and it is not within your capacity to do it either.

First be selfish, first transform yourself. Your life in peace, in joy, in health, can be a great source of nourishment for people who are starving for spiritual food.

People are not really starving for material things. Material richness is very simple: just a little more technology, a little more science, and people can be rich. The real problem is how to be inwardly rich. And when you are outwardly rich you will be surprised — for the first time you become more acutely, more keenly aware of your inner poverty. For the first time all meaning in life disappears when you are outwardly rich, because in contrast, the inner poverty can be seen more clearly. Outside there is light all around and inside you are a dark island.

The rich man knows his poverty more than the poor person, because the poor person has no contrast. Outside there is darkness, inside there is darkness; he knows darkness is what life is. But when there is light outside you become desirous of a new phenomenon: you long for inner light. When you see that richness is possible outside, why can't you be rich inside?

[23] FREEDOM

Free yourself from attachment.

If you don't cling to anything, how can you be made miserable? Your clinging creates misery, because you want to cling and in the very nature of things, things are changing; you cannot cling. They are slipping constantly out of your hands. There is no way to cling to them.

You cling to the wife, you cling to the husband, to the children, to the parents, to the friends. You cling to persons, to things, and everything is in a constant flux. You are trying to hold a river in your arms and the river is flowing fast; it is rushing towards some unknown goal — you are frustrated.

The wife falls in love with somebody else — you are frustrated. The husband escapes — you are frustrated. The child dies — you are frustrated. The bank fails, goes bankrupt — you are frustrated.

The body becomes ill, weak, death starts knocking at the door — you are frustrated. But these frustrations are because of your expectations. You are responsible for them.

If you understand that this place is not a home and you are a homeless wanderer here, a stranger in an unknown land and you will have to leave, you will have to go... if you have penetrated that point, if you have understood it, then you don't make a home anywhere. You become a homeless wanderer, a *parivrajaka*. You may even literally become so; it depends on you. You may really become a wanderer, or spiritually you may become a wanderer.

My own emphasis is not to become literally a wanderer, because what is the point? Buddha's emphasis was not on becoming literally a wanderer; let it be clear to you. Buddha has not said what to do, whether to follow him literally or not. Millions followed him literally — they dropped out of their homes, out of their families; they really became *bhikkhus* wandering all over the country, begging.

If really you understand then there is no need to do it in such a factual way. You can be in the home, you can be with your wife and your children and yet remain alert that nothing belongs to you. Remain alert that you don't fall into attachments; remain alert that if things change you are ready to accept the change, that you will not weep for the spilt milk, that you will not cry, that you will not go crazy and mad. To me this seems to be more significant than really becoming a wanderer.

Understanding it deep in your awareness is enough. My emphasis is to become a spiritual wanderer. There is no need to drag the body like a beggar; just let your spirit be that of a wanderer, and that is enough. Don't create bondage for your spirit.

[24] OVERCOMING

With gentleness overcome anger.
With generosity overcome meanness.
With truth overcome deceit.

Meditation is an alchemical process — it is not morality, it is alchemy. It is the science of the soul. Through meditation anger slowly slowly disappears, and its energy becomes available and becomes gentleness.

You will be surprised to know that if you suffer from great anger you have great potential for gentleness. Anger simply shows that you have great energy. A man without anger is impotent, he has no energy. A man who cannot be angry cannot be gentle either.

With generosity overcome meanness. Don't repress meanness, don't destroy meanness, but with generosity transform it into a generous consciousness, into sharing.

With truth overcome deceit. Don't fight with darkness, bring light in. That is the essence of this sutra. Don't fight with the negative, bring the positive in. And the positive comes through watchfulness — the negative is already there. Your society prepares you for the negative, your society needs you to be negative. Your society wants you to be angry, full of anger, so that you can be forced into war, into crusades: religious, political, ideological conflicts; so you can be manipulated into killing people. Or, you can be manipulated into becoming martyrs; destructive to yourself.

Never fight with the negative. Your society prepares you for the negative. Transform the negative into the positive. Transformation is possible. The medium that has to be used is meditation.

[25] BEYOND SORROW

*The wise harm no one. They are masters of their
bodies and they go to the boundless country.
They go beyond sorrow.*

And who is wise? Not the one who knows much, but the one who understands much. The wise is not one who has all the scriptures at the tip of his tongue; the wise is one who has seen his own reality, and seeing it has become aware of the universe and its beauty and its intelligence. The wise is one who has seen the wisdom of existence; he is not knowledgeable, but he is absolutely innocent. How can he harm anyone? — that is impossible, because he can't see others as different from himself. He sees the whole as one.

Beware of knowledgeable people, beware of the so-called experienced, they are not wise.

Two women were sitting in the doctor's waiting room, comparing notes on their various disorders.

"I want a baby more than anything in the world," said the first, "but I guess it's impossible."

"I used to feel just the same way," said the second, "but then everything changed. That's why I'm here; I'm going to have a baby in three months."

"You must tell me what you did!"

"I went to a faith healer."

"But I have tried that. My husband and I went to one for nearly a year and it didn't help a bit."

The other woman smiled and whispered, "Try going alone next time, dear."

The experienced people, the people who have lived life... they appear wise; they are not wise, they are only mature fools. And mature fools are more dangerous than the immature fools, because the mature fool has all the arguments to support his foolishness, all his experience is at his disposal.

The professor of criminal law was concluding his final lecture before the holidays. "Remember, gentlemen, if you have an affair with an underage girl, with or without her consent, it is rape! If you have an affair with a girl of age without her consent, that is rape; but if you have an affair with a girl of age with her consent, Merry Christmas!"

These people are wise in a way, wise in the ways of the world; they can give you good advice, but they are not wise in the sense Buddha uses the word. They are as foolish as you are, just a little bit more experienced.

[26] THE YELLOW LEAF

> You are as the yellow leaf.
> The messengers of death are at hand.
> You are to travel far away.
> What will you take with you?

There are two things in life that are the most important. The first is birth, and the second is death — everything else is trivia. The first has already happened, now nothing can be done about it. The second has not happened yet, but can happen any moment. Hence those who are alert will prepare, they will prepare for death. Nothing can be done about birth, but much can be done about death. But people don't even think about death, they avoid the very subject. It is not thought to be polite to talk about it. Even if they refer to death, they refer to it in roundabout ways. If somebody dies, we don't say that he has died. We say God has called him, that God loved him so much, that whomsoever God loves he calls earlier. That he has gone to heaven, that he has moved to the other world, that he has not died, only the body has fallen back to the earth but the soul, the soul is immortal.

Have you ever heard of anybody going to hell? Everybody goes to heaven. We are so afraid of death, we try to make it as beautiful as possible: we decorate it, we speak beautiful words about it, we try to avoid the fact.

But Buddha insists again and again... his whole life after his enlightenment for forty-two years continuously he was talking, morning, evening, day in, day out, year in, year out, about death. Why? Many people think that he is a pessimist — he is not. He is neither optimist nor pessimist. He is a realist, he is very pragmatic. He means business, because he knows only one thing is left for you about which something can be done and should be done — and that is death.

We talk about everybody who dies — that he has gone to heaven, that he has become a beloved of God, that God has chosen him, called him forth... ways of avoiding death.

But Buddha talks continuously about death. He says: *You are as the yellow leaf.* The yellow leaf represents death. Any moment it is going to fall down, dust unto dust. Any moment and death is going to possess you. Tomorrow may never come, even the next moment is not certain. This is the only moment you can be certain of, the next moment you may not be here. What are you doing to prepare for that great journey into the unknown?

Death is powerful, but one thing it cannot take away from you — that is meditation. If you can become rooted in your being — alert, conscious, watchful — you will see that you are not the body, and you are not the mind, and you are not the heart. You are simply the witnessing soul, and that witnessing will go with you. Then you can witness even death. That witnessing is the source of all religiousness. Those who have attained to that source are the enlightened ones, are the buddhas.

[27] TRAVEL ON ALONE

He does not linger with those who have a home nor with those who stray. Wanting nothing, he travels on alone.

In India, people are divided into two categories; this is a tradition. It was so in Buddha's time too, it is a very ancient division. Buddha is trying to make a distinction. He is trying to make his disciples a third category — the ancient categories are two. The first is the worldly, the householder, those who have a home. They are called householders for the simple reason that they live in the fallacy of security, safety — a safety that they think comes through money, power, prestige, a security that they think comes out of relationships. The wife thinks she is safe with the husband, the husband thinks he is safe with the wife, the parents think they are safe with their children. The safety is fallacious because neither the family nor money nor anything else of this world can save you from death.

When death comes it shatters everything; it shatters all your sand-castles. The householder lives in a kind of dream world, a world of his own projections. It is not true, it does not correspond to reality;

it is his own projection. The wife thinks the husband is her security and the husband thinks the wife is his security. Now, both are insecure. How can two insecure persons give security to each other? Two insecure persons together become doubly insecure, but the fallacy is created. This is the first category, the *grihastha*, the householder.

And the second category is of those who have renounced the first category, who have moved to the other extreme — who don't live in houses, who don't live in families, who don't earn money, who don't even touch money, who have moved to exactly the opposite extreme. They are known as *sannyasins*. They used to wander around the country in small or big groups.

But Buddha says, "You have dropped a small family and now you have moved into a bigger crowd — you have become another family. Nothing has changed. First you were thinking the small family was your security, now you think this crowd of monks is your security, but the old idea of security still persists."

He says that to be a *sannyasin* means to accept the natural insecurity of life. That very acceptance is *sannyas* — to accept that, "I am born alone and I will die alone, and between these two alonenesses all ideas of being together with somebody are just fantasies. I am alone even while I am alive." One is born alone, one lives alone, one dies alone.

Buddha's emphasis is very much on the fact of your aloneness; he wants you to be aware of it. Once you are aware of it you will be surprised at the beauty of it, at the joy of it. You will not be scared; you will rejoice in it because it has a freedom, it has an ecstasy in it, it has a purity and innocence in it. And why hanker for security?

Life is insecure in its very nature, hence it is simple logic: those who want to be more alive, they have to live in insecurity. The greater the insecurity, the more will be your aliveness; the greater the fallacious, so-called security, the less will be your aliveness.

That's why you see so many dead people in the world, almost dead, for the simple reason that they have become so attached to the idea of security. And the more dead you are, the more secure you are. Don't do anything that can create any insecurity, remain confined to the familiar, don't ever go beyond the limits. You will never know the ecstasy of going beyond the limits. You will never know the ecstasy of exploring the unknown and the unknowable.

According to Buddha, both categories are the same people. Of course they are extremists and they appear opposite to each other, but don't be deceived. They are not really opposite; they have found different kinds of security.

Wanting nothing, he travels on alone — the real *sannyasin* has no desire, not even desire for life; hence he is not afraid of death. He has no desire in this world or in the other; hence he is not concerned with creating all kinds of safeties around himself. He is not concerned. He can be alone, utterly alone. He is not trying to be clever and cunning with existence; he trusts existence. He can see that the householders are living in a projection, in a projected world of their own; and the so-called monks and nuns are living in another projection, but again it is a projected world. He moves alone — it has not only to be an outward act, it has to be an inward feeling also.

To be alone is the most fundamental thing for a meditator — to experience aloneness, to sit silently and just be yourself, just be with yourself, not hankering for any company, not hankering for the other. Enjoy your being, enjoy your breathing, enjoy your heartbeat. Enjoy the inner accord, the harmony. Enjoy just that you are, and be utterly silent in that enjoyment.

[28] DO YOUR WORK

Live in love. Do your work.
Make an end of your sorrows.

A Buddha is a creator, a Jesus is a creator. Their words, their acts are the only proof that God exists. Their very presence is proof that God exists. Their presence is creative; in their very presence thousands of people are transformed. Buddha is not an escapist; he cannot be. No awakened person can be an escapist. Cowards escape, courageous people are creative.

He is not against love, he is not against creativity, and he is not against work either. Do your work — because unless you do the work that is close to your heart you will remain unfulfilled. And the meditator finds immediately what his work is. The meditator finds intrinsically that this is his work; he does not have to think about it. It is so clear and so loud that he knows that he has to be a musician or he has to be a poet or he has to be this or that. It comes so clear that there is no question of doubt. And then he starts working; that work is his meditation.

There are many people who are afraid of work. They don't know that there is a type of work that is totally different from the work that you have come across in your life, and that work can be a meditation.

And if you can drop your willfulness, your ego, then hatred also drops because hatred is nothing but the shadow of your ego. If there is no ego there is no hatred; if there is ego, there is always hatred following it. Whosoever comes in the way... and everybody will come in the way because egos cannot adjust to each other. Egos are always in conflict, egos are always quarreling, they are quarrelsome, hence the hatred.

Drop the ego and see the beauty of egolessness. Then there is no hatred, no anger. You become so silent, your energy becomes so calm and quiet, that suddenly you start seeing the world in a different light, in a different perspective. Then this ordinary world is no longer ordinary — it becomes sacred.

[29] NOT IN THE SKY

The way is not in the sky.
The way is in the heart.

Look within. Watch how many jealousies, how many angers, how many lustful desires are boiling there. Just watch them!

And this is the greatest contribution of Buddha — that he has said, and proved beyond doubt because it has worked for thousands of people — that a deep observation of anything that is wrong in you is enough; you need not do anything else. Just be aware of it and it disappears. It disappears just as you bring light into a room and the darkness disappears.

Become aware, awake. Then you will see that everything comes and goes, all things come and pass. Life is a flux. Your consciousness is the only thing that is immovable, that is eternal. To attain it is freedom. To attain it is the goal of life.

[30] AWAKE FOREVER

> All things arise and pass away.
> But the awakened awake forever.

Life can be lived in two ways: either as a continuous fall... then you are pulled by the unconscious forces of gravitation; you need not make any effort. You are not trying to reach to the peaks, you are simply a rock rolling downwards. Naturally it appears easy, comfortable, convenient. If you conform with the society, if you live according to the tradition, if you follow the crowds, life is easy — but at a very great cost. You don't grow. You miss the whole point, because life is significant only when it is a continuous growth.

Man is the only animal in existence who has the capacity to evolve. Charles Darwin says that monkeys have evolved and become men. I don't agree with him, I can't agree with him. Not that I have anything against the monkeys — they are good people! — but if what he says is true, then why have not all the monkeys become men? For millions of years monkeys have remained monkeys. Why are they not growing? They should have taken at least a few preliminary steps by now, but they are exactly the same as they have always been.

You can find proofs for Charles Darwin's theory only if you watch the politicians. Then one suspects he may be right — otherwise not! Otherwise, monkeys have remained monkeys.

In fact, Darwin's whole theory is only a guess; it is not yet scientifically valid. And spiritually it is never going to be valid, because those who have known man's spiritual growth have come decisively to this conclusion: that man is a different being altogether from any other being on the earth. He is an evolving animal. No other animal evolves; they remain the same. They are very conformist: they don't go beyond their heredity. They never cross the limit of what is allowed by their instincts; they never do anything beyond the instinctive, beyond the unconscious.

It is only man who has been able to produce a Buddha, a Lao Tzu, a Jesus, a Bahauddin. It is because of the buddhas that we can say man has the capacity to be a God. Man has an infinite potential.

But then you cannot live an easy life. You cannot just be a Rotarian or a Lion. You can't be just a Hindu or a Mohammedan. You can't go on following the crowds. Crowds behave instinctively; they don't know anything of the beyond. Their life is easy. If you are part of them your life will also be easy, but there will be no growth. And growth is all that matters.

The only thing that matters in life is growth. Unless you are moving to the ultimate peak of becoming a God you are wasting a tremendous opportunity.

[31] THE WAY OF THE LAW

> If you determine your course with force
> or speed, you miss the way of the law.

The ego is always aggressive; it can exist only through aggression. It creates such fuss, such dust, such smoke, that you can't see. It makes you blind. It whirls you round and round, it makes you dizzy. That's why the ego is always hankering for more and more power, more and more force. It wants to do things with absolute force.

The ego is a fascist, it is totalitarian, it is dictatorial. It does not want any rebellion against itself. It immediately destroys any possibility

of you becoming free of it. Just the seed of a rebellion... and it starts destroying it. It is constantly watching. It is constantly trying to keep you so occupied that you never become aware of the great slavery you are living in. And the ego is very cunning: it convinces you that "I am you."

So whenever the idea of dropping the ego arises you start feeling as if you are losing your identity. The ego is not your identity. It is because of the ego that you are not able to know who you really are. The ego is the barrier. It keeps you running and it keeps you at such a speed, in such a hurry, that you don't have any time to think things over, to ponder, to meditate, to see what you are doing and why you are doing it.

It does not give you any time to see. It keeps you crazy, engaged, constantly engaged in one desire or other. Before one desire is spent it creates ten more. It keeps new desires ready so there is never a gap, never an interval left between two desires — because in that gap you will be able to see and recognize the stupidity of your life, the utter madness of your life. And once you have seen it you cannot remain part of it anymore. You will jump out of it! You have seen that the house is on fire.

Buddha says: *If you determine your course with force or speed, you miss the way of the law.* You miss the whole point of existence, because existence is available in all its beauty and benediction only to those who are living in a relaxed way. Not with force, not with any speed; not rushing, running. It is available to those who are at rest, at home with the present moment, so relaxed as if there is no other time. This moment is all....

If you go with speed you will miss; if you are in too much of a hurry you will not be able to see. Your eyes will remain clouded, you will remain tense. You will not be able to see that which is, because your mind is so full of desire, of ambition, of achievement, you can't see that which is. You are always hankering for that which should be.

Ordinarily, the "ought" has become more important than the "is," the "should be" has become more important than "that which is." And existence is that which is, truth is that which is.

[32] WITHOUT HASTE

Quietly consider what is right and what is wrong. Receiving all opinions equally, wihtout haste, wisely, observe the law.

When Buddha says "quietly consider" he means don't think — drop all thinking and see. That is the only way to know things as they are... because if you are thinking, you are bringing your prejudices in. If you are thinking, you are bringing your past conclusions in. If you are thinking, your mind is functioning — and mind is past, and the past never allows you to see the present. Thinking has to stop for meditation to be. Thinking has to evaporate totally. In that state of no-thought you can see.

Buddha says: Meditate quietly. Be silent and see. And in that seeing you will know — without any logical process you will simply know: This is this. This is good and this is bad. Not that you have to decide it according to the Bible or the Koran or the Gita. If you have eyes you know where the wall is and where the door is. Do you have to think about it? Each time you go out of your room do you have to think again and again where the door is and where the wall is?

You simply go out of the door without thinking at all, because you can see! But if you are blind, each time you will have to think again, "Where is the door?" You will have to grope for the door.

Thinking is a blind state, it is a groping in darkness. Meditation is a state of having eyes, you are capable of seeing. You simply see what is right and what is wrong. And when you see what is right and what is wrong you can't do the wrong, you can't go against the right.

A meditator naturally follows that which is good — not that he decides to follow it — and naturally avoids that which is bad. Not that he decides to avoid it; a meditator never takes any vows — there is no need. A man with eyes never takes the vow that "I will always enter from the door, go out from the door. I promise you, God, that I will never try to enter from the wall. Believe me, I am a man of my word, I will keep it, although I know there will be many temptations." If somebody is saying that, you will laugh. "What nonsense he is talking! What temptations?" Have you ever been tempted by the wall to get in and out through it? No such temptation is there.

Buddha says, "receiving all opinions equally" — without any prejudice, without any opinion already arrived at…. Just listen to, and watch, all kinds of things. Be a pure mirror — that is meditation. And without haste, because if you are in a hurry you will jump upon the conclusion. You are not really concerned with truth, you are more concerned with a conclusion, because the conclusion gives comfort, the conclusion gives you a security, the conclusion makes you feel that you know. It covers up your ignorance, it makes you feel sure and certain.

Hence people are so ready to become part of any church. They are not ready to become free. Even if sometimes they leave a church, they leave only to join another church. The Hindu becomes the

Mohammedan, the Mohammedan becomes the Christian, the Christian becomes the Hindu. And this way they go on moving from one church to another, but they remain the same people because their approach remains the same.

Without haste, wisely, observe the law. Don't be in a hurry. In hurrying you may decide something which is not true. Just for the longing to make a decision, you may conclude, you may start believing. A real inquirer is ready to wait, he is very patient. Even if it takes lives he is ready to devote lives.

Truth is worth devoting as much time to as you can.

[33] LOVING AND FEARLESS

Be quiet,
and loving and fearless.

Three things Buddha says: Be quiet — learn to be silent more and more — and loving, because if your silence is not loving it will make you insensitive. Then your silence will be that of a cemetery — dull, dead. It will not be a silence which can celebrate, it will not be a silence which can sing and dance. It will not be a silence which can bloom in a thousand and one flowers. Hence, Buddha immediately says: it should be loving.

And love is possible only if you are fearless; if you are afraid you cannot be loving. The man who is afraid of anything — death, the police, the magistrate, the government — the man who is afraid of anything can't love.

And all fears are basically fears arising out of death. The fear of the policeman is also the same, because he can kill, he can shoot you. The fear of the government is nothing but the fear of violence — the government can kill more powerfully than anybody else. What is the fear of the magistrate and the law? — because the magistrate has the power to send you to the gallows or he can give you a life sentence. You are afraid. But deep down all fear is of death... and death is a myth. It has never happened, it never happens, it is never going to happen.

The meditator comes to know the falsity of death, and in that very moment all fear disappears; he becomes fearless. When you are fearless you are neither a coward nor brave, because both are rooted in fear. The coward has succumbed to fear and the brave is trying to win over fear, but both are concerned with fear. And the fearless one has simply dropped the whole thing. He is neither brave nor cowardly. He knows there is no death, there is nothing to be afraid of and there is nothing to be brave about.

This is a different dimension, a transcendence of the duality of cowardice and bravery.

Be fearless, be loving, be silent, and you will be wise.

[34] SILENCE

Silence cannot make a master out of a fool.

This is a strange statement from a buddha, because silence has been praised so much; but the buddha says the truth as it is. He does not care about the tradition.

In India, silence has been one of the most praised qualities for centuries. The Jaina monk is called *muni* — *muni* means "the silent one." His whole effort is to be silent, more and more silent. Buddha says, "But don't be a fool, just silence is not going to help." It may help you keep your foolishness to yourself, but the foolishness will go on accumulating, and sooner or later it will be too much. It is bound to come out, and it is better to let it come out in small doses every day rather than accumulating it, and then having it come like a flood.

This has been my observation, too. The people who have remained silent for a long time become very stupid, because their silence is only on the surface. Deep down there is turmoil. Deep down they are the same people, with greed, jealousy, envy, hatred, violence — unconscious, with all kinds of desires. Maybe now they are desirous of the other world, greedy for the other world, thinking more of paradise than of this world and the earth. But it is the same thing, projected onto a bigger screen, projected on eternity. In fact, the greed has grown a thousandfold. First it was for small things: money, power, prestige. Now it is for God, samadhi, nirvana. It has become more condensed and more dangerous.

Then what has to be done? If silence cannot make a master out of a fool, then what can make one a master? Awareness. And the miracle is, if you become aware, silence follows you like a shadow.

But then that silence is not practiced; it comes of its own accord. And when silence comes of its own accord, it has a tremendous beauty to it. It is alive, it has a song at its innermost core. It is loving, it is blissful. It is not empty; on the contrary, it is a plenitude. You are so full that you can bless the whole world and yet your sources remain inexhaustible; you can go on giving, and you will not be able to exhaust the source. But it happens through awareness.

That is Buddha's very significant contribution, his emphasis on awareness. Silence becomes secondary, silence becomes a by-product. One does not make silence a goal — the goal is awareness.

[35] SWEET TO BE FREE

Look within—the rising and the falling.
What happiness! How sweet to be free!

Buddha brings a totally new vision of meditation to the world. Before Buddha, meditation was something that you had to do once or twice a day, one hour in the morning, one hour in the evening, and that was all. Buddha gave a totally new interpretation to the whole process of meditation. He said: This kind of meditation that you do one hour in the morning, one hour in the evening, you may do five times or four times a day, is not of much value. Meditation cannot be something that you can do apart from life just for one hour or fifteen minutes. Meditation has to become something synonymous with your life; it has to be like breathing. You cannot breathe one hour in the morning and one hour in the evening, otherwise the evening will never come. It has to be something like breathing: even while you are asleep the breathing continues. You may fall into a coma, but the breathing continues.

Buddha says meditation should become such a constant phenomenon; only then can it transform you. And he evolved a new technique of meditation.

His greatest contribution to the world is Vipassana; no other teacher has given such a great gift to the world. Jesus is beautiful, Mahavira is beautiful, Lao Tzu is beautiful, Zarathustra is beautiful, but their contribution, compared to Buddha, is nothing. Even if they are all put together, then too Buddha's contribution is greater because he gave such a scientific method — simple, yet so penetrating that once you are in tune with it, it becomes a constant factor in your life.

Then you need not do it; you have to do it only in the beginning.
Once you have learned the knack of it, it remains with you; you need
not do it. Then whatsoever you are doing, it is there. It becomes a
backdrop to your life, a background to your life. You are walking,
but you walk meditatively. You are eating, but you eat meditatively.
You are sleeping, but you sleep meditatively. Remember, even the
quality of sleep of a meditator is totally different from the quality of
the sleep of a nonmeditator. Everything becomes different because
a new factor has entered which changes the whole gestalt.

Vipassana simply means watching your breath, looking at your
breath. It is not like the *pranayama* of Yoga. It is not changing your
breath to a certain rhythm, with deep breathing, or fast breathing.
No, it does not change your breathing at all; it has nothing to do with
the way you breathe. Breathing is only used as a device to watch,
because it is a constant phenomenon in you. You can simply watch it,
and it is the most subtle phenomenon. If you can watch your breath
then it will be easy for you to watch your thoughts.

One thing immensely great that Buddha contributed was the
discovery of the relationship between breath and thought. He was the
first man in the whole history of humanity who made it absolutely clear
that breathing and thinking are deeply related. Breathing is the bodily
part of thinking and thinking is the psychological part of breathing.
They are not separate, they are two aspects of the same coin. He is the
first man who talks of bodymind as one unity. He talks for the first time
about man as a psychosomatic phenomenon. He does not talk about
body and mind, he talks about bodymind. They are not two; hence no
"and" is needed to join them. They are already one — bodymind — not
even a hyphen is needed; bodymind is one phenomenon. And each
body process has its counterpart in your psychology and vice versa.

Meditators come across a point: When the mind really completely ceases, breathing also ceases. And then great fear arises. Don't be afraid — many meditators have reported to me, "We became very much afraid, very much frightened, because suddenly we became aware that the breathing has stopped." Naturally, one thinks that when breathing stops death is close by. It is only a question of moments, you are dying. Breathing stops in death; breathing also stops in deep meditation. Hence deep meditation and death have one thing similar: in both, the breathing stops.

Therefore, if a man knows meditation he has also known death. That's why the meditator becomes free of the fear of death: he knows breathing can stop and still he is. Breathing is not life; life is a far bigger phenomenon. Breathing is only a connection with the body. The connection can be cut — that does not mean that life has ended. Life is still there; life does not end just by the disappearance of breathing.

Buddha says: Watch your breathing; let it be normal, as it is. Sitting silently, watch your breath. The sitting posture will also be helpful; the Buddha posture, the lotus posture, is very helpful. When your spine is erect and you are sitting in a lotus posture, your legs crossed, your spine is aligned with the gravitational forces, and the body is at its most relaxed state. Let the spine be erect and the body be loose, hanging on the spine — not tense. The body should be loose, relaxed, the spine erect, so gravitation has the least pull on you.

Hence the lotus posture is something valuable. It is not just a body phenomenon; it affects the mind, it changes the mind. Sit in a lotus posture — the whole point is that your spine should be erect and should make a ninety-degree angle with the earth. That is the point where you are capable of being the most intelligent, the most alert, the least sleepy.

And then watch your breath, the natural breath. You need not breathe deeply. Don't change your breathing; simply watch it as it is. But you will be surprised by one thing: the moment you start watching, it changes — because even the fact of watching is a change and the breathing is no longer the same.

Slight changes in your consciousness immediately affect your breathing. You will be able to see it — whenever you watch, you will see your breathing has become a little deeper. If it becomes so of its own accord it is okay, but you are not to do it by your will. Watching your breath, slowly slowly you will be surprised that as your breath becomes calm and quiet your mind also becomes calm and quiet. And watching the breath will make you capable of watching the mind.

That is just the beginning, the first part of meditation, the physical part. And the second part is the psychological part. Then you can watch more subtle things in your mind — thoughts, desires, memories.

And as you go deeper into watchfulness, a miracle starts happening: as you become watchful less and less traffic happens in the mind, more and more quiet, silence; more and more silent spaces, more and more gaps and intervals. Moments pass and you don't come across a single thought. Slowly slowly, minutes pass, hours pass....

And there is a certain arithmetic in it: if you can remain absolutely empty for forty-eight minutes, that very day you will become enlightened, that very moment you will become enlightened. But it is not a question of your effort; don't go on looking at the watch because each time you look, a thought has come. You have to again count from the very beginning; you are back to zero. There is no need for you to watch the time.

[36] THE SHINING WAY

Everything arises and passes away.
When you see this, you are above sorrow.
This is the shining way.

The way of Gautama the Buddha is the way of intelligence, understanding, awareness, meditation. It is not the way of belief, it is the way of seeing the truth itself. Belief simply covers up your ignorance; it does not deliver you from ignorance. Belief is a deception you play upon yourself; it is not transformation.

And the people who think themselves religious are only believers, not religious. They have no clarity, no understanding, no insight into the nature of things. They don't know what they are doing, they don't know what they are thinking. They are simply repeating conventions, traditions, dead words spoken long, long ago. They cannot be certain whether those words are true or not. Nobody can be certain unless one realizes oneself.

There is only one certainty in existence and that is your own realization, your own seeing. Unless that happens, don't be contented; remain discontented. Discontentment is divine; contentment through beliefs is stupid. It is through divine discontent that one grows — but it is an arduous path. The path of belief is simple, convenient, comfortable. You need not do anything. You have only to say yes to the authorities: the authorities of the church, of the state. You have simply to be a slave to people who are in power.

But to follow the path of Buddha one has to be a rebel. Rebellion is its essential taste; it is only for the rebellious spirit. But only rebellious people have spirits, only they have souls. Others are hollow, empty.

These sutras of today are of immense beauty, truth. Meditate over them:

Everything arises and passes away.
When you see this, you are above sorrow.
This is the shining way.

It is a very strange world. Everything is momentary, yet every momentary thing gives you the illusion of being permanent. Everything is just a soap bubble, shining beautifully in the sunrays, maybe surrounded by a rainbow, a beautiful aura of light — but a soap bubble is a soap bubble! Any moment and it will be gone and gone forever. But for the moment it can deceive you.

And the strangest thing is that thousands of times you have been deceived, yet you don't become aware. Again another soap bubble and you will believe. Your unintelligence seems to be unlimited! How many times do you need to be hammered? How many times do your dreams have to be crushed and shattered? How many times has life to prove that clinging is nonsense? Stop clinging and then you go beyond sorrow. It is clinging that is the root cause of sorrow.

Buddha says: *Everything arises and passes away. When you see this....* He is not saying, "Believe this." He is not saying, "I have become the enlightened one, so whatsoever I say you have to believe in it." He is not saying, "Because scriptures are in my favor you have to believe me." He is not saying, "Because I can prove it logically you have to believe in me."

See the beauty of the man. He says: *When you see this, you are above sorrow.* In that very moment when you have seen this — that everything is momentary and everything is a flux and everything is bound to change.... Do whatsoever you want to do, but nothing is going to become permanent in this life. When you have seen this with your own eyes, and you have understood it through your own intelligence, suddenly you are beyond sorrow.

What happens? A great revolution happens in that seeing; that very seeing is the revolution. Then you don't cling. The moment you see that this is a soap bubble you don't cling to it. In fact, clinging to it will force it to burst sooner; if you don't cling to it, it may remain there dancing in the wind for a while. The nonclinger can enjoy life; the clinger cannot enjoy life.

If you see, you can enjoy; then it is just a game. Then everything is totally different; then it is a big drama. Then the whole earth becomes just a stage and everybody is acting his part.

Look around. Everything is changing. It is like a river moving and moving — and you want to catch hold of it? It is mercury! If you try to catch hold of it you will lose sooner than before. Don't try to catch hold of it. Watch joyfully, silently. Witness the game, the dream... and you are above sorrow.

[37] THE WAY OF BRIGHTNESS

> Existence is sorrow.
> Understand, and go beyond sorrow.
> This is the way of brightness.

Sorrow arises out of clinging to momentary things that you cannot make permanent. It is not in the nature of things. It is against the universal law. It is against *dhamma*, it is against Tao. You cannot win. If you fight with the universal law you are fighting a losing battle; you will simply waste your energies. What is going to happen is bound to happen; nothing can be done about it.

All that you can do is about your consciousness. You can change your vision. You can see things in a different light, with a different context, in a new space, but you cannot change things. If you think of the world as very real you will suffer; if you see the world as a strange dream you will not suffer. If you think in terms of static entities you will suffer. If you think in terms of nouns you will suffer. But if you think in terms of verbs you will not suffer.

Nouns don't exist. They exist only in languages; in reality there are no nouns. Everything is a verb because everything is changing and everything is in a process. It is never static, it is always dynamic.

The second thing Buddha says is, "Existence is sorrow." To be is sorrow. The ego is sorrow. First he says: See the world as dream, fluctuating, changing, moment to moment new. Enjoy it, enjoy its newness, enjoy all the surprises that it brings. It is beautiful that it is changing, nothing is wrong about it; just don't cling to it.

Why do you cling? You cling because you have another fallacy: that you are.

The first fallacy is that things are static, and the second fallacy is that you are, that you have a static ego. They go together. If you want to cling you need a clinger; if you have no need to cling, there is no need for a clinger. Go deep into it: If you don't need to cling, the ego is not needed at all, it will be pointless. In fact, it cannot exist without clinging.

The dancer can exist only if he dances. If the dance disappears, where is the dancer? The singer exists only in singing. The walker exists only in walking. So is the ego: the ego exists only in clinging, in possessing things, in dominating things. When there is no domination, no desire to dominate, no desire to cling, no desire to possess, the ego starts evaporating. On the outside you start clinging and in the inside a new clarity starts arising. The ego with all its smoke disappears, the ego with all its clouds disappears. It can't exist because it cannot be nourished anymore. For it to exist it has to cling. It has to create "my" and "mine," and it goes on creating "my" and "mine" in every possible and impossible way.

The "I" exists only as an island in the ocean of "my" and "mine." If you stop claiming things as "my" and "mine," the ego will disappear on its own accord.

Neither the wife is yours nor the husband nor the children. All belongs to the whole. Your claim is foolish. We come empty-handed into the world and we go empty-handed from the world. But nobody wants to know the truth — it hurts. Empty-handed we come and empty-handed we go. One starts feeling shaky, one starts feeling scared. One wants to be full, not empty. It is better to be full of anything — any garbage — than to be empty. Emptiness looks like death, and we don't want the truth. Our whole effort is to live in convenience, even if that convenience is based on illusions.

"I demand an explanation and I want the truth!" shouted the irate husband upon discovering his wife in bed with his best friend.

"Make up your mind, George," she calmly replied. "You can't have both."

Either you can have the explanation or the truth. And people are more interested in the explanation than in the truth, hence so many philosophies. They are all explanations — explanations to explain away things, not to give you the truth; explanations to create great smoke so you need not see the truth. And Buddha's insistence is that you see it — because without seeing it you can't go above sorrow.

[38] WORDS

Master your words.

Ordinarily a mind is full of words — relevant, irrelevant, rubbish; all kinds of words go on gathering inside you. Two persons are talking; you simply hear, and those words become part of your mind — for no other reason, accidentally. You heard two persons talking. You have become burdened. You go and you read the signboards, and those words become part of your being. You read unnecessary advertisements. In magazines, people read advertisements more than anything else. Or you go on gossiping with people, knowing perfectly well that this is just useless, a sheer wastage of time and energy. But words are gathering inside you like dust, layers upon layers, and your mirror will be covered by them

Buddha says, *Master your words.* Be telegraphic. Listen only to that which is significant, read only that which is meaningful. Avoid the unnecessary, the irrelevant. Speak only that which is to the point. Make your each word your heart. Don't just go on saying things as if you are a gramophone record.

Mary was sitting alone on the couch when her mother came in and turned on the light.

"Why, what is the matter, dear?" asked her mother. "Why are you sitting here in the dark? Did you and John have a fight?"

"Oh, no, nothing like that," replied Mary. "As a matter of fact, John asked me to marry him."

"Well, then why do you look so sad?"

"Oh, mother, it is just that I don't know if I could marry an advertising executive."

"But what is wrong with marrying a man who is in advertising?"

"Well, how would you feel if a man who was proposing to you told you that it was a once-in-a-lifetime, never-to-be-repeated, special offer?"

Just like a gramophone record! He may not be at all aware what he is saying, may be repeating his habit. He is skillful in that, it has become part of his mind. It may be repeating itself; he may not be conscious at all of what he is doing.

When Buddha says, "Master your words," he means be conscious. Why are you saying something? To whom? And what is the purpose of it? Be clear, otherwise be silent.

[39] THOUGHTS

Master your thoughts.

Any thought goes on inside your mind. Watch for a few minutes and you will be surprised: the mind seems to be crazy! It jumps from one thought to another thought for no reason at all. Just a dog starts barking in the neighborhood and your mind takes the clue from it... and you remember the dog that you used to have in your childhood, and the dog died... and you start feeling sad. And because of the death of the dog you start thinking about death, and the death of your mother and the death of your father. And you become angry because you were never at ease with your mother; there was always conflict. The dog is still barking, completely unaware what he has done. And you have traveled so far!

Anything can trigger a process in you. This is a kind of slavery:

you are at the mercy of accidents. This is not mastery. And a sannyasin, a seeker, should be a master. He thinks only if he wants to; if he does not want to think he simply puts his mind off. He knows how to put it on and how to put it off.

You don't know how to switch it on, you don't know how to switch it off; it goes on and on. It starts working in the childhood and goes on working till you die. Seventy years, eighty years, continuously working — so much work, and then you cannot expect anything great out of it because it is utterly tired. It has not much energy left; it is leaking from everywhere. If you can switch it off... that's what meditation is all about: switching the mind off, the art of switching the mind off. If you can switch it off, it will gather energy.

If for a few hours every day you are without the mind, you will gather so much energy that that energy will keep you young, fresh, creative. That energy will allow you to see reality, the beauty of the existence, the joy of life, the celebration. But for that you need energy.

[40] GIDDY AND DISTRACTED

> Death overtakes the man who, giddy and
> distracted by the world, cares only for his flock
> and his children. Death fetches him away
> as a flood carries off a sleeping village.

The great advances in medical science have given us the idea that we are going to live forever. Medical science has certainly helped us to live a little longer than before, but that simply means a little longer: the same misery, the same desire, the same lust, the same bondage.

Medical science may be able to extend life. It seems very possible now that man may start living more than one hundred years on average. There are people who think that people can live at least three hundred years very easily. But what is the point? Whether you live seventy years or seven hundred years, you will be the same stupid person. In fact, in seven hundred years your stupidity will grow very much! And if death is postponed for seven hundred years, who cares? It is not going to happen soon... and humankind does not have enough insight to look that far.

We live surrounded by small things. We see only so far, just a little bit ahead, enough to walk. Seven hundred years... that will make religions disappear from the earth, because man is not so intelligent that he can be aware of death if death is postponed for seven hundred years. He is not even intelligent enough to see it after seventy years, not to mention seven hundred years.

I have seen people who are seventy and yet not interested in meditation. Strange, very strange. I can't believe it. A man of seventy is still not interested in meditation? That simply means he has not yet been able to see death, and death is very close. Any moment it can happen.

Buddha wants you to remember death continuously. Don't think that he is a pessimist. Don't think that he is death-obsessed — no, not at all. He simply wants you to remember death so that the sword of death hanging on you keeps you aware, alert.

[41] FOREVER BOUND

If you are happy at the expense of another man's happiness, you are forever bound.

From the very beginning we start poisoning every child with the poison of competitiveness. By the time he comes out of the university he will be completely poisoned. We have hypnotized him with the idea that he has to fight with others, that life is a survival of the fittest. Then life can never be a celebration. Then life can never have any kind of religiousness in it. Then it cannot have any quality of sacredness. Then it is all mean, ugly.

Buddha says: If you are happy at the expense of another man's happiness, you are forever bound.

Naturally. If you are happy at the expense of another man's happiness — and that is how you can be happy, there is no other way. If you find a beautiful woman and somehow manage to possess her, you have snatched her away from others' hands. We make things look as beautiful as possible, but that is only the appearance. Now the others who have lost in the game, they are angry, they are in a rage. They will wait for their opportunity to take revenge, and sooner or later the opportunity will be there.

Whatsoever you possess in this world you possess at somebody else's expense, at the cost of somebody else's pleasure. There is no other way. If you really want not to be inimical to anybody in the world, you have to drop the whole idea of possessiveness. Use whatsoever happens to be with you in the moment, but don't be possessive. Don't try to claim that it is yours. Nothing is yours, all belongs to existence.

We come with empty hands and we will go with empty hands,

so what is the point of claiming so much in the meantime?

But this is what we know, what the world teaches us: possess, dominate, have more than the others have. And it may be money or it may be virtue; it does not matter in what kind of coins you deal — they may be worldly, they may be otherworldly, but be very clever, otherwise you will be exploited. Exploit and don't be exploited — that is the subtle message given to you with your mother's milk. And every school, college, university, is rooted in the idea of competition.

A real education will not teach you to compete; it will teach you to cooperate. It will not teach you to fight and come first. It will teach you to be creative, to be loving, to be blissful, without any comparison with the other. It will not teach you that you can be happy only when you are the first. That is sheer nonsense. You can't be happy just by being first. And in trying to be first you go through such misery that you become habituated to misery by the time you become the first.

A real education will not teach you to be the first. It will tell you to enjoy whatsoever you are doing, not for the result but for the act itself. Only then can existence flow through you. Only then can it use your hands and your fingers and your brush. Only then something of superb beauty can be born.

It is never *by* you but only *through* you. Existence flows; you become only a passage. You allow it to happen, that's all; you don't hinder, that's all.

Don't think of the result at all. Just do what you are doing with your totality. Get lost into it. Lose the doer in the doing. Don't "be" — let your creative energies flow unhindered.

[42] LONG IS THE ROAD

And for the wanderer, how long is the road wandering
through many lives! Let him rest. Let him not suffer.
Let him not fall into suffering.

And how long have you been wandering! When are you going to decide to be awake? You have slept long enough. It is time to wake up and to start a totally new kind of life which is lived from inside. Light a flame inside of awareness, and then wherever you are it is all joy.

You need rest, you have wandered enough. You are tired, utterly tired, weary, bored.

The time is right now. Don't suffer anymore. Don't fall again and again into suffering. To fall into forgetfulness is suffering; to remember is to come out of suffering. And rest is the most necessary step for remembering, for awareness. Relaxation is the whole art of meditation and bliss both.

How can you rest with so many desires? They go on pulling you apart. You can rest only if you learn the secret of desirelessness; if you learn to live moment to moment without any future; if you learn to live without any hope for the future; if you live concentratedly in the present, totally involved in the moment, neither worried by the past nor worried by the future, relaxed, at rest. Then meditation and bliss both are easy, a spontaneous growth out of a restful heart, out of a relaxed being.

[43] SIT. REST. WORK.

Zazen means just sitting doing nothing. The first thing to do is learn sitting, a deep restfulness. Become a pool of rest, not even ripples of desire, going nowhere, no ambition — not even for God, not even for nirvana.

Sit... not only physically — psychologically, spiritually too. Learn to sit; that is Zazen. And rest — and fall into a deep rest, so the breathing becomes natural, the body becomes cool, all the fever of constant desire and turmoil disappears, evaporates.

And then, work. That work will have a totally different quality. It won't be out of desire; it will be creativity. It will be because you have so much energy available that you would like to share your energy with the world, that you would like to create something, that you would like to make the world a little more beautiful, a little more blissful, a little more human.

Sit. Rest. Work.

Let these three words sink deep in your heart. Learn to sit silently, restfully, not fighting with yourself, relaxed. Not in a yoga posture, remember, because the yoga posture is a constant effort. No yoga posture is needed. Sit in any way that you find relaxed — even a chair will do.

Buddha used to sit on the floor; that was easy in those days. You can sit in any posture you like. You can use a pillow, a Zen pillow, to sit upon; you can use a chair. The question is not the posture; the question is inner rest.

Be at rest... and when energy accumulates in you, start being creative. Paint, sing, dance, or do whatsoever you feel like doing to make this world a little more beautiful, a little more warm.

We have to create a paradise on the earth.

[44] DUST ON THE ROAD

> *Do what you have to do resolutely,*
> *with all your heart. The traveler who hesitates*
> *only raises dust on the road.*

Buddha says: *Do what you have to do resolutely....* But by resolution he does not mean will, as it is ordinarily meant in the dictionaries. Buddha is compelled to use your words, but he gives a new meaning to his words. By 'resolution' he means out of a resolved heart — not out of willpower but out of a resolved heart. And remember, he emphasizes the word 'heart', not the mind. Willpower is part of the mind. A resolved heart is a heart without problems, a heart which is no longer divided, a heart which has come to a state of stillness, silence. That's what he calls a resolved heart.

Do what you have to do resolutely, with all your heart. Remember the emphasis on the heart. Mind can never be one; by its very nature it is many. And the heart is always one; by its very nature it cannot be many. You cannot have many hearts but you can have many minds. Why? — because the mind lives in doubt and the heart lives in love. The mind lives in doubt and the heart lives in trust. The heart knows how to trust; it is trust that makes it one. When you trust, suddenly you become centered.

Hence the significance of trust. It does not matter whether your trust is in the right person or not. It does not matter whether your trust will be exploited or not. It does not matter whether you will be deceived because of your trust or not. There is every possibility you may be deceived — the world is full of deceivers. What matters is that you trusted. It is out of your trust that you become integrated, which is far more important than anything else. It is not a question that first you have to be certain whether the person is worthy of trust or not. How will you be certain? And who will inquire?

It will be the mind, and the mind knows only how to doubt. It will doubt. It will doubt even a man like Christ or Buddha. It can't help itself.

So remember, trust does not mean that first you have to inquire, that first you have to make everything certain, guaranteed, and then you trust. That is not trust, that is really doubt: because you have no more possibilities to doubt, hence you trust. If another possibility arises of doubt you will doubt again. Trust is in spite of all the doubts, in spite of what the man is or what the man is going to do. It is of the heart, it is out of love.

When you trust and love with a resolved heart it brings transformation. Then you never hesitate. Hesitation simply keeps you in fragments. Taking a quantum leap, without any hesitation or in spite of all the hesitations, you become integrated. Hesitations disappear; you become one. And to become one is to be liberated — liberated from your own stupid crowd that exists inside you, liberated from your thoughts and desires and memories, liberated from mind itself.

[45] QUIETEN YOURSELF

If you cannot quieten yourself, what will you ever learn? How will you become free?

Face life and its questions and its realities on your own, even if your own responses are not so great — they cannot be. Of course you cannot respond like a buddha, but by borrowing some answer from Buddha you will never be intelligent enough to become a buddha yourself. Yes, you will commit many errors, many mistakes. Yes, you will go astray many times — go, don't be worried! Life is meant for that, so that you can try. It is through trials, many errors, many mistakes, that one learns. When you learn by your own efforts you become intelligent. And only an intelligent person can see the beauty of meditation, can understand the significance of meditation.

If you cannot quieten yourself, what will you ever learn?

And all learning happens through meditation; it does not happen through study. That is accumulation of information, it is not learning. Always be alert about borrowed knowledge: howsoever precious it appears it is all false, pseudo — for you. It is not pseudo for the man who has lived it. It is true for Buddha, true for Jesus, true for Krishna, but not for you. You will have to live....

Buddha also had the scriptures available. He could have read Krishna; the Gita was available. And he was well-educated — he was the son of a king. All the scriptures must have been available to him and great scholars and great teachers were available to him. He could have recited the Gita every day; he could have learned the Gita so absolutely that he would have been able to repeat it just from memory, but then he would have missed buddhahood.

And in Krishna's time also the Vedas were available, but Krishna did not borrow knowledge from the Vedas. In Jesus' time the Old Testament was available, but Jesus tried to find out the truth for himself. This is something very essential to understand: truth has to be found by oneself. Only then is it liberating; otherwise it becomes a bondage — a beautiful bondage, but a bondage all the same.

And if you cannot learn.... How will you become free?

It is only by experiencing truth on your own that freedom happens. Freedom is the fragrance of the experience of truth.

[46] THE TRUE WAY

See what is. See what is not.
Follow the true way.

Gautama the Buddha has given to the world the most psychological religion. It is incomparable; no other religion even comes close to it. Its heights, its depths, are tremendous. And the reason why Buddha succeeded in giving such a beautiful vision of life is very simple: he did not believe; he inquired, he explored. He did not believe in the tradition, he did not believe in the scriptures, he did not believe in the priests.

This was one of his fundamentals: that unless *you* know, you don't know. You can borrow knowledge, you can become knowledgeable, well informed, a scholar, a pundit, a professor, but you will not be a seer. Deep down the ignorance will persist and will affect your life. Deep down you will remain the same childish self, immature, ungrounded, uncentered, unintegrated. You will not be an individual, you won't have any authenticity. You will be pseudo, false, phony.

It is a quantum leap into the unknown. When you don't believe in the tradition, when you don't believe in the scriptures, when you don't believe in anything except your own experience, you are going into the unknown all alone. It needs guts, it needs courage. And only a courageous person can be truly religious.

Cowards are there in the churches, in the temples, in the mosques in millions, but they don't create any religious beauty, any religious fragrance in the world. They don't make the world more beautiful, more alive, more sensitive. They don't create anything.

They only go on doing formalities, rituals. They themselves are dead and they go on deceiving others; they themselves are deceived.

Borrowed knowledge creates great deception because you start feeling as if you know — and that "as if" is a big "as if."

Truth liberates, belief binds. Truth liberates because it has to be yours; it has to be an inner experience, an encounter with that which is.

Buddha is a nonbeliever. He is not an atheist like Karl Marx or Friedrich Nietzsche; neither is he a theist like all the priests of all the religions. He is an agnostic. He neither believes nor disbelieves; he is open. That is his great gift to the world: to be open to truth.

Go utterly naked, without any conclusions, without any ideology, any prejudice. Otherwise there is every possibility that you will project your own idea. You will not see that which is, you will see only that which you want to see. You will be creating your own reality which is bound to be false. Reality has not to be invented, it has to be discovered. It is already there. And remember, it is not the reality which is hidden, it is your eyes which are covered with layers of dust.

Buddha gave to the world a nonmetaphysical religion, a psychological religion. He simply helps you to go beyond mind. He helps you to understand the mind because it is only through understanding that transcendence happens.

[47] TO LIVE ARDUOUSLY

It is sweet to live arduously, and to master yourself.

We are not living arduously. We are not trying to climb new mountains, new peaks. We are not trying to explore. We have become more concerned with comfort, with security, safety.

Buddha says: *It is sweet to live arduously.*

Have you ever enjoyed climbing to the peak of a mountain? It is hard. You perspire, breathing becomes difficult, you become tired. And then you reach to the sunlit peak and then you lie down on the grass, and what relaxation and what joy arises in your being! The silence of the peak and the arduous climb, and you have reached, and the joy of reaching! You could have been dropped by a helicopter, but then there would have been no joy. It would have been comfortable.

Edmund Hillary could have reached to the peak of Everest by a helicopter — it would have been easier — but he tried the hard way. And he writes, "I have never known such bliss. When I reached to the peak I was all alone, the first man on Everest." Nobody had seen the sky from that point, nobody had seen the world from that point. It was sheer ecstasy. He danced.

Sooner or later buses will be going there and hotels will be there and cinema houses, and it will become very comfortable. But don't hope that you will have the same ecstasy as Edmund Hillary had, although you will be standing on the same spot. You will look a little silly and stupid, that's all. And you will not believe why this Hillary danced; you don't see any point. All around there are hotels and tourist centers and guides and everything is available; the whole

world is there. You don't see why he laughed, why he enjoyed, why he danced, because you don't feel any dance.

Life is joy only when you live it raw, when you live it in all its wildness, when you live it naturally, spontaneously. Yes, there are bound to be difficulties, there are bound to be dangers, but they are part of life, and without them life will not be life at all. And this is the only way to master yourself.

[48] WISDOM IS SWEET

And wisdom is sweet, and freedom.

Gautama the Buddha does not talk about God, but he talks about love, freedom, truth, authenticity. He talks about the essential religion. He does not waste his breath on heaven and hell, the theory of reincarnation. He is absolutely unconcerned about the so-called great metaphysical problems. He is nonmetaphysical — in a sense, very down to earth. He means business. He wants to give you a science which can transform your life. He is interested in creating an alchemy of inner revolution so the base metal can be changed into gold. His religion is unique, in a way.

There are three types of religions in the world. Jainism is the only religion which is emphatically atheistic. It denies God and raises man to his ultimate peak. It declares that man is God and there is no other God. Except Jainism, all other religions — Hinduism, Judaism, Islam, Christianity — are theistic. They are rooted in the idea of God; without God they will be at a loss what to do. They are at a loss because since Nietzsche declared "God is dead," humanity, by and by, has agreed with Nietzsche. His statement became very prophetic; it represents the twentieth-century mind. And the religions that have depended on the idea of God for centuries feel uprooted. They are dying, withering away.

Buddha is unique. He is neither atheistic like Jainism, nor theistic like other religions. He is a superb agnostic. He says there is no need to worry about unnecessary things. Think of the essential, think of the intrinsic, and don't be bothered about the accidentals.

If you are authentic, if you are compassionate, if you are meditative, then if there is a God he will come to you; you need not go in search for him. And if there is a paradise it will descend in your heart. There is no need to be bothered about such abstract ideas; they simply waste your time. And if you are not authentic, not meditative, not compassionate, not wise enough, even if you come across God what are you going to do? You will feel a little embarrassed and God will feel a little embarrassed facing you. You both will be unnecessarily in a strange situation — what to say, what to do, what not to say, what not to do. You would like to escape and he would like to escape.

Just think: if suddenly you come across God, what will you do? You will run away from him as fast as you can!

Buddha simply cuts all your hoping and desiring. He does not say there is no God, he does not say there is. He simply says it is irrelevant. What matters is your inner transformation, and the inner transformation cannot be postponed for tomorrow; it can happen right now.

That's the trouble with Buddha: if you go with him you have to drop your hopes, you have to drop your desires. You have to be in the present, utterly silent. And then life has a new color, a new joy, a new music. Then life has a new beauty.

[49] BE FREE

*In all things be a master of what you do and
what you say and think. Be free.*

Freedom is the ultimate goal of true religion — not God, not paradise, not even truth, but freedom. This has to be understood because this is Gautam Buddha's essential message to the world. Freedom is the highest value according to him, the summum bonum; there is nothing higher than that. But by freedom he does not mean political freedom, social freedom, economic freedom. By freedom he means the freedom of consciousness.

Our consciousness is in a deep bondage; we are chained. Inside is our prison, not outside. The walls of the prison are not outside us; it exists deep in our unconscious. It exists in our instincts, it exists in our desires, it exists in our unawareness.

Freedom is the goal.

Awareness is the method to reach that goal.

And when you are really free you are a master; the slavery disappears. Ordinarily we may appear free, but we are not free. It may appear that we are the choosers, but we are not the choosers. We are being pulled, pushed by unconscious forces.

When you fall in love with a woman or a man, do you think you have decided it, it is your choice? You know perfectly well you cannot choose to love, you cannot force yourself to love somebody. You are not the master, you are just a slave of a biological force. That's why in all the languages the expression is 'falling in love' — you fall in love: you fall from your freedom, you fall from your selfhood. If love were your choice you would rise in love, not fall in love. Then love would be out of your consciousness, and it would have a totally different quality, a different beauty, a different fragrance.

The ordinary love stinks — stinks of jealousy, anger, hatred, possessiveness. It is not love at all. Nature is forcing you towards something which is not of your choice; you are just a victim. This is our slavery. Even in love we are slaves, what to say about other things? Love seems to be our greatest experience; even that consists only of slavery, even in that we only suffer.

People suffer more in love than in anything else. The greatest suffering is that it deludes you — it creates the illusion that you are the chooser, and soon you know that you are not the chooser; nature has played a trick upon you. Unconscious forces have taken possession of you, you are possessed. You are acting not on your own; you are just a vehicle. That is the first misery that one starts feeling in love, and one misery triggers a whole chain of misery.

Soon you become aware that you have become dependent on the other, that without the other you cannot exist, that without the other you start losing all sense of meaning, significance. The other has become your life, you are utterly dependent; hence lovers continuously fight, because nobody likes to be dependent, everybody hates dependence. Nobody likes to be possessed by somebody else because to be possessed means to be reduced to a thing. The whole humanity suffers for the simple reason that every relationship goes on reducing you, goes on making your prison smaller and smaller.

Buddha says: This life is not true life. You are being lived, you are not really living. You are being lived by unconscious forces. Unless you become conscious, unless you take possession of your own life, unless you become independent of your instincts, you will not be a master. And without being a master there is no bliss, no benediction; life remains a hell.

[50] ABANDON YOUR SORROWS

> O slave of desire, float upon the stream.
>   Little spider, stick to your web,
> or else abandon your sorrows for the way.

People find it very difficult to abandon their sorrows. It looks, on the surface, somehow not right. Why should people hesitate to abandon their sorrows for the way?

But it is the most difficult thing to abandon your sorrows because you have lived with them for so long, you are so friendly with them, and to live with the familiar sorrows feels so cozy, so warm — old friends, and to abandon them.... And suddenly all your walls will disappear and you will be under the open sky because your walls consist of nothing but your sorrows. Your prison will disappear! — and you have lived in the prison for so long, for so many lives that it has become your home.

Many prisoners, whenever they are released from prison, will be back within three or four months; they will do something and they will be back in the prison. I used to visit prisons and I asked a few people who were returning again and again to prison, "What is the matter?"

They said, "When we leave the prison it feels as if we are leaving our home! We have lived in here so long and all our friends are here." One man said, "Not only my friends but my whole family is here! Outside I am just a stranger and I start feeling homesick, so I have to do something and come back."

Once a person is imprisoned it is very rare that he will not come back again. He will come back again because the prison gives some security, some safety. You need not bother, you need not worry about tomorrow. At the right time the food will be provided, at the right time you will go to bed, at the right time you will be awakened in the morning. Life is so disciplined — like a monastery!

In fact, monasteries and prisons are not very different, just the names are different. Monasteries are a little harder, that's all! Prisons are a little more human. And modern prisons, particularly in the developed countries, are really worth living in, with color television and everything!

Man has been improving continuously for centuries — he has improved his prisons very well! He has become very sophisticated, cultured, civilized, and this is nothing but just painting the prison walls, making them beautiful. And now suddenly a Buddha comes and says to you, "Come out in the open. Abandon your miseries, your sorrows"? You cannot abandon your miseries and sorrows so easily.

That's why people who leave the world, renounce the world, create new miseries of their own. If there is nobody else to create misery for them — if you don't have a wife to create it, if you don't have a husband to create it, if there is nobody to support you in your misery — you will create it yourself. People are sleeping on beds of thorns... now, no wife prepares it, they themselves work hard on it! People are fasting, almost killing themselves. Now, nobody is doing it to them, that is their own idea.

The ascetics are self-destructive; they are suicidal people, masochistic, perverted, but they are worshipped. They are worshipped because they create their own misery! You worship people as saints, as mahatmas, if they create their own misery. They should be entered into mental asylums, they should be treated! They need medical care. They are not mahatmas, they are simply masochists. They have renounced the world, but they cannot renounce misery so they start creating their own misery. And when a person creates misery for himself, you all respect him. You have been told that this is something great; he is sacrificing his life for God.

God is not a sadist. He does not enjoy your miseries and your sorrows. Don't be foolish, don't be stupid! But the reason is that people cannot abandon their miseries. They can renounce the gold and the palaces and the money and the power, they can renounce everything, but when it comes to renouncing the miseries, this becomes the most difficult thing they encounter, because miseries have been with you so long that you don't know any other style of living. The only style that you have become accustomed to is sorrow.

[51] LEST YOU DISTURB YOUR QUIETNESS

Do not turn away what is given you,
nor reach away what is given to others,
lest you disturb your quietness.

Don't become knowledgeable. Even if you have come to know yourself, don't become knowledgeable. Even if you have encountered God, don't become knowledgeable. Whatsoever you have known, forget all about it. Become again innocent. Remain always in the state of not-knowing, then much more will go on happening to you.

What ordinarily happens when you move into meditation is that something happens, but you don't feel grateful; on the contrary, you feel this is your due — in fact it should have happened long ago. You are such a worthy person, so virtuous, so holy, and you have done so much; why should you be grateful?

That is a wrong approach; that means you are stopping the process. In gratefulness much more will come to you. So even if a little glimpse comes to you, feel grateful. Just a ray of light and feel grateful, as if the whole sun has come to you. And the whole sun will be coming, following the ray. But if you are not grateful you become closed; even the ray will disappear and you will again be in your darkness, back in your darkness.

[52] WATCH

Quieten your mind.
Reflect. Watch.

Contemplate over these sutras. Try to experience them... because Buddha is not an ordinary religious person. He is not interested in miracles. He is not interested in anything occult, esoteric. He is interested in transforming you. He is very down to earth.

Moses and Jesus were playing a round of golf at the Celestial Country Club. First, Jesus teed up and made a hole in one. Then Moses also drove a hole in one.

"Well, Moe, we are even so far," said Jesus.

"Now look here, Jake," Moses protested. "We made our point. Now what do you say we cut out the miracles and play a little golf?"

Buddha never did any miracles — that is the greatest miracle. He is not interested in mystifying you. His whole effort is to give you the key so you can open the doors of all the mysteries. He is very existential, nonphilosophical, nonintellectual in his approach. He is not heady — but very practical, pragmatic. His whole approach is experimental, experiential. So you will not be able to understand him if you only go on reading.

Try to experiment with what he is saying. Try to quieten your mind, reflect, watch, and see yourself what happens: freedom, bliss, truth, wisdom, innocence, purity... thousands of flowers start blooming in you. The spring suddenly bursts forth.

SAMMASATI — DISCOVERING THE BUDDHA

In a single word,
everything significant is contained:
Sammasati.

Gautam the Buddha is not the only buddha in the history of the world; there have been thousands of buddhas around the world, in different parts of the world. They may not be known as buddhas, but buddha simply means "the awakened one."

The word *buddha* simply means the awakened one. It was not Gautam Buddha's name; his name was Gautam Siddharth. When he became awakened, those who understood his enlightenment started calling him Gautam Buddha. But the word *buddha*, according to Gautam Buddha too, is simply inherent in every human being, and not only in every human being, but every living being. It is the intrinsic quality of everybody. Everybody has the birthright to become a buddha.

Anybody awake, anywhere in the world, has the right to be called a buddha. Gautam Buddha is only one of the millions of buddhas who have happened and who will happen.

The only quality the buddha at the center of being has is watchfulness, witnessing. Witnessing is the whole of spirituality compressed into one word. Witness that you are not the body, witness that you are not the mind, and witness that you are only a witness. Just a mirror reflecting — without any judgment, without any appreciation, without any condemnation — a pure mirror. That's what the buddha is.

Being a buddha is not being a Buddhist. A Buddhist is a follower,
a buddha knows.

The moment you know your own buddhahood you have come
to know all the buddhas; the experience is the same.

Be silent. Close your eyes.
Look inwards as deeply as possible.
This is the way.
At the very end of the way, you are the buddha.

And the journey is very short — a single step.
Just total urgency and absolute honesty is needed
to look straight into your own being.
There is the mirror; the mirror is the buddha.
It is your eternal nature.
Deeper and deeper, you have to go in
until you find yourself.
Don't hesitate. There is no fear.
Of course you are alone,
but this aloneness is a great, beautiful experience.
And on this path you will not meet anyone except yourself.

Relax, and just be a watchful, witnessing mirror,
reflecting everything.
Neither do those things have any intentions to be reflected,
nor do you have any intention to catch their reflections.
Just be a silent lake, reflecting, and all bliss is yours.
This present moment becomes no-mind, no-time,
just a purity, a space unbounded.

This is your freedom.

And unless you are a buddha, you are not free.
You know nothing of freedom.
Let this experience sink deep
in every fiber of your being.
Get soaked, drenched.
When you come back, come back drenched
with the mist of your buddha nature.
And remember this space, this way,
because you have to carry it out twenty-four hours
in all your actions.
Sitting, standing, walking, sleeping,
you have to remain a buddha.
Then the whole existence becomes an ecstasy.

About the Author

For over thirty years Osho has spoken to thousands of people about everything from contemporary social problems to the essential themes that unite the world's great wisdom traditions.

He discourses with eloquent familiarity on virtually all the world's great mystics including Zen masters, Hassids, Sufis, Bauls, Buddha, Lao-Tzu and Jesus. The message is aimed at rebels and risk takers - people who consider themselves intelligent, adventurous, and independent, and want to be more so.

No one is more qualified to introduce these mystics than Osho. He speaks from his own experience, bringing his mystic predecessors to life and making them contemporaries.

One of the key insights in the Osho approach to the fulfillment of the human spirit is what he calls "Zorba the Buddha," a person who can dance with feet happily on the ground, while the hands are touching the stars. Zorba represents the human love affair with the earth and all its flowers, greenery and mountains, the rivers and oceans. Buddha represents our longing to reach the sky with all its stars, rainbows, and the freedom of the passing clouds. An integrated individual, who represents a synthesis of East and West, of the inner and the outer, the spiritual and scientific, of the sacred and the mundane, is Osho's hope for humanity as a whole.

The material for this Buddha Discovery Deck comes from a series of twelve volumes of transcribed talks by Osho on the *Dhammapada* — the essential works of Gautama the Buddha.

for more information visit:

www.osho.com

ALSO BY OSHO

The Book of Secrets

Osho Zen Tarot

Meditation: The First and Last Freedom

Courage: The Joy of Living Dangerously

Creativity: Unleashing the Forces Within

Maturity: The Responsibility of Being Oneself

Osho Transformation Tarot

Autobiography of a Spiritually Incorrect Mystic

Love, Freedom, and Aloneness

Intuition: Knowing Beyond Logic

Awareness: The Key to Living in Balance

Intimacy: Trusting Oneself and the Other

Yoga: The Science of the Soul

Tao: The Pathless Path

Zen: The Path of Paradox

Art of Tea — Meditations to Awaken your Spirit